KEEPER OF THE STORIES

A Motivational Guide for Older Beginning Writers

by

Heidi Hartwiger

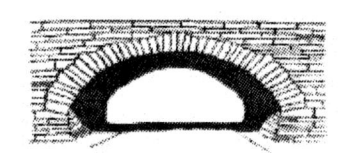

Parkway Publishers, Inc.
Boone, North Carolina
2002

Copyright © 2002 by Heidi Hartwiger
All Rights Reserved

Available from:

Parkway Publishers, Inc.
P. O. Box 3678
Boone, North Carolina 28607
Telephone/Facsimile: (828) 265-3993
www.parkwaypublishers.com

Library of Congress Cataloging-in-Publication Data

Hartwiger, Heidi.
    Keeper of the stories : a motivational guide for older beginning writers / by Heidi Hartwiger.
       p.   cm.
ISBN 1-887905-59-6
1. Authorship. I. Title.
PN147 .H344 2002
808'.06692--dc21
2002002922

Editing and Typesetting: Schuyler Kaufman
Cover Design: Aaron Burleson, Spokesmedia.com

Table of Contents

INTRODUCTION	vii
Chapter One: RESET THE COMPASS	1
Chapter Two: THE HISTORIAN'S APPROACH	11
Chapter Three: FINDING GOOD STORIES	21
Chapter Four: A WRITER'S JOURNAL	33
Chapter Five: THE EXPERIENCE OF OTHERS	43
Chapter Six: TAMING WILD THOUGHTS	57
Chapter Seven: ANECDOTE TO STORY	75
Chpter Eight: NARRATIVE NIGHTMARES	85
Chapter Nine: GREAT BEGINNINGS AND ENDINGS	95
Chapter Ten: SPEAK TO ME	109
Chapter Eleven: SHOW DON'T TELL	125
Chapter Twelve: DONATIONS TO THE WORD BANK	139
APPENDIX	145

Peace is liberty in tranquility.
Cicero

ACKNOWLEDGEMENTS

**Without the support and encouragement
of these people
this book would still be in my heart.**

Farideh Goldin, Doris Gwaltney, Luisa Igloria, Lee and Harriet Kennedy, Martha Benn MacDonald, Carolyn Rhodes, and my SELU Sisters of Radford.

Colleagues and friends from
Christopher Newport University

Stevalynn R. Adams,
Graphic Artist

Lisa M. Curry,
Director of the Center for Community Learning

Jane B. Sulzberger,
Coordinator for the LifeLong Learning Society

**The enthusiastic and helpful members of the
LifeLong Learning Society**

Thank you, my friends!

For My Keeper of the Stories

JANE GREER KRAUSE

A Message from the Author to the Reader

Several years ago I was offered the opportunity to teach a class about writing life stories.

This was an interesting addition to my fiction and creative nonfiction courses at the Center for Community Learning and the LifeLong Learning Society of Christopher Newport University. Members of the LifeLong Learning Society must be fifty-five or older to belong, so many of my adult students are retired and want to begin writing projects such as genealogy, family histories, and family stories. Teaching the life stories classes has proven to be a challenge and an interesting change from traditional writing classes. As I prepared, I realized there was very little material that addressed my needs or those of my classes, so I created my own materials.

I realized no matter what genre they select, older beginning writers have unique writing needs. They excel at the critical analysis of an essay, and when dealing with short stories, they understand the parts of a plot. However, when they write, they carefully craft their sentences to the point that they run out of creative steam. The work is never completed because of word-by-word, sentence-by-sentence tinkering. Many can talk out their thoughts to form a story, but they have little confidence in their writing skills. Some procrastinate when it comes to putting pen to paper.

Because new students arrive with each semester, I like to take an informal survey to make certain that I understand and meet their needs. The following are typical concerns:

> I have trouble developing one small idea into a full story.
>
> I am a procrastinator so getting started is a real problem.
>
> If I could just get a satisfactory first sentence, then I could write.
>
> I don't know if I have enough information to write a family story.
>
> How do you write a good beginning to a story?
>
> I am not sure that I have something to write about or that I can even write.
>
> How can you write dialogue if the person has been dead a long time?

Class by class I create materials to address their writing concerns and needs. In addition to dialogue, moving from active to passive voice, redundancy, adverb abuse, and "showing not telling" seem to be major writing bugaboos for beginning older writers.

Keeper of the Stories is based on information gathered and successfully used as course material. I, the aging hippie, still try to make the world be a brighter place. My vision for the book extends far beyond its usefulness in the classroom. It is a multipurpose book to entertain and to encourage intergenerational communication. In addition, *Keeper of the Stories* can serve as a guide for Elderhostel writing workshops, and as a writing resource for program directors at retirement communities.

This book is written for and with the help of my LLS students. I thank the many students who urged me to create this book, and I also thank the students who graciously offered their work as examples to emphasize specific points. I believe reading work by other older beginning writers encourages and motivates. I have watched my students become discouraged after reading a "perfectly perfect" piece. While not completely flawless, the student writing in this volume provides entertaining models and reinforces specific topics.

Do not expect this small volume to be a traditional text about the writing process. It is an anecdotal guide to motivate older beginning writers. There is a smattering of practical strategies such as how to collect and organize material for family stories, how to turn an anecdote into a story, how to write and punctuate dialogue, and how to revise without spending all your creative energies in the process.

Every family has a "keeper of the stories." Sooner or later that person accepts the role, and the writing begins. This book is written with love, laughter, and support for all those reluctant "keepers of the stories" whose time has now come.

Heidi Hartwiger
2002

Notes

CHAPTER ONE:
Reset the Compass

Some of us from the Bob Dylan generation have etched in our hearts his raspy voice of protest chanting to us about how "the times they are a-changing." Dylan's words have come to pass. The times are changing. No more rocking chair, slippers and lap robe for the retiree. While some people might want to shop until they drop, not many folks these days choose to work until their last gasp. In general, people are retiring earlier, while still in good health, with plenty of "get up and go."

Some folks yearn for the ultimate tourist experience now that they have time for travel; others learn to play a musical instrument, or become more involved with leisure sports such as golf, tennis, or swimming. No matter what is selected from the free-time buffet the following words are certain to be familiar: "When I retire, and I WILL retire early, I'll finally have time to do the things I want to do. The first thing I will do is travel, or I could get prints made from those slides and organize albums, and then again I just might have time to jot down those family stories told and retold at holiday gatherings."

The odds are that you have entertained these thoughts, spoken these words at least once, or at the very least, on occasion perceived their reverberations throughout the Baby Boomer crowd. Maybe you came of age as I did in the 1960s and know already that LIFE is a trip! We are vintage people with stories to tell.

Recalling a tender, sad, or thigh-slapping-funny moment is an unspoken promise we make to ourselves. Then what happens? We get busy, and the moment is lost. We forget! But be of good cheer, that moment may be lost but not gone forever. It could be a birth, graduation or marriage announcement, or a reunion, an old hat, the big fish, or a postcard collection which stirs the sleeping memory.

Witness the growing market for memory books, which really are glorified scrapbooks. Superstores, specialty shops, and crafts outlets devote much shelf space to stickers, borders, and decorative theme sheets to assist the preparation of an eye-catching album. It is interesting to note that very little space is dedicated in these colorful binders to recording the actual stories of the memorable happenings. Down the road the pictures with snappy captions remain; however, the details and other "good stuff" for retelling the event may fade as memory does.

As you plunge into time travel (which is exactly what you will do as you shape your stories), as you gather and tell stories of the family, you will begin the trip of all trips, the strange and interesting trip of reviewing, and in some cases reviving, memorable times, good and bad. Consider this book as a compass to give you direction while you chart your course through the writing maze. You have motivation; maybe you have actually collected materials for a humdinger of a family scrapbook filled with stories; but you still struggle with an overload of jumbled ideas that refuse to come into focus. You could be a beginning writer who believes in a great idea but somehow lacks perseverance and fails to commit that idea to paper, even the simple pages of a memory book.

It was when Eleanor Hill retired from a career in family counseling that she reset her compass as she began to consider pursuing new interests. She joined LifeLong Learning Society, which offers a variety of educational courses and cultural activities based at Christopher Newport University in Newport News, Virginia. She registered for my writing class, and after several sessions, she shared her thoughts with me about why she began to write:

> I have frequently wondered about writing for enjoyment or if I could write well enough for others to enjoy what rattles around in my head. The opportunity never arose, or I never could justify taking the time and effort to write.
>
> Now that my children are grown, and I no longer am employed, I decided I would take the risk and try a writing course. Fortunately for me, I got into your class and with your encouragement have begun writing little stories from my childhood life experiences.
>
> I also took a risk and joined a storytelling group and have become a Teller. I use the stories I have written to tell and have been very pleased with the results. Finding out that I can write stories and then use them to tell has been a gift to myself.

Whether you write poetry or prose, fiction or nonfiction you will find early on that writing is a rewarding journey. Do you remember the classic children's tale of The Red Shoes? Once the shoes were on the feet, the dancing began and continued until the dancer dropped from exhaustion or the shoes came off. So it is with gathering and writing family stories. One must start somewhere, so usually there is a clearly defined beginning, but for as long as the writer is willing to gather and write, there seems to be no definitive end. Telling your stories or those of another can be a small jaunt, which leads to an extended tour of the past.

At other times stories are a voyage, a pilgrimage towards the future. Other LifeLong Learners have commented that writing not only helps explain personal detours in the journey, but also helps to piece together the life puzzles of long departed family members. Robert Kelly, a retired naval architect and marine engineer, reflected similar thoughts as he discussed why he writes:

> At some point in our lives we wonder who we are and where we came from. While my parents told me much about my family, I now find great gaps that I cannot bridge because there is no one alive to explain them. I also think back to all the conversations between my parents and other adult family members and the things I could not comprehend because I was too young or inexperienced to understand. There were also people they simply did not talk about. It has left me with a confusing legacy.
>
> When my children get to the point of wondering who they are and where they came from, I want them to have all the family stories and myths that I can put to paper to give them the broadest

possible view of the Kelly, Ramthun and Haslett families. I want them to know all the funny things, the hurtful things, the sad things and the humdrum things that I can recall. This also helps me to understand better what happened and why my people became what they were. Finally, it helps me to know who I am and when I came from. And so I write.

Yet another LifeLong Learner, Bob Jones, writes not so much about family but of his adventures and misadventures while in the United States Navy during World War II. His is a refreshing voice speaking of the less grim aspects of wartime. Not only did the footloose young sailor have any eye for adventure, but he also had a great appreciation for the pretty girls he met at every port. Jones has converted many of his experiences as a young sailor into essays, which have appeal across the generations. In one essay Jones discussed love letters and contemplated where all those love letters he wrote to the pretty girls in every port have gone.

Perhaps you are familiar with Jesse Stuart, writer, poet, and teacher from Kentucky, who celebrated life's stories in much of what he wrote. Stuart drew from his teaching experiences as he composed many of his short stories. Additionally, Stuart wrote of his family who lived along the Big Sandy River in the mountains of eastern Kentucky. Many believe after completing *God's Oddling*, Stuart considered that book to be "the harvest of all his writing seasons." It seems through *God's Oddling*, stories of his father, mother and family, Stuart was able to respect and reflect on the past and concurrently contemplate the future as senior writers such as Ms. Hill, Mr. Kelly, and Mr. Jones have begun to do.

Occasionally, writing is sojourning in the present. Writing a family story was not in my thoughts as I was "in the moment," wrapping a birthday gift, my treasured, well-used teapot, which had been in the family for as long as I could remember. The gift was for Jenifer Emily, my adult daughter.

Then it hit me! My great Aunt Emily, Jenifer Emily's namesake, once owned the teapot. I remembered Aunt Emily pouring tea from that dusty-rose colored teapot. My daughter, unlike some of the twenty something crowd, reveres tradition. I believe the teapot would have greater significance if she knew more about the owner and the passion that woman had for a good cup of carefully brewed tea.

And so the Emily stories began. I had old photos copied, and located a postcard from Europe written in her familiar bold hand to go with the stories. I even found the little demitasse spoon used by Emily to give her namesake, her infant great-great-grandniece, the first sip of tea.

Do you see how easily a story which wasn't, suddenly happens? At the outset, it may be as unclear to you, as it was to me, which direction your reset life compass will send you. That is a challenge, not a problem. If you are to write, you must embark upon the writing journey. If you are to create stories of your family, you already have plenty of eclectic "baggage" which will be either lost in transit or evolve into a quintessential collection of stories.

Even before the teapot episode, my life changed as I reset my compass. After the last of my four children left home, I began my challenging writing excursion. I left high school teaching and moved to adult education. Although I enjoyed teaching writing classes in the continuing education setting at Rappahannock Community College in Glenns, Virginia, and later at

Christopher Newport University's Center for Community Learning, my writing horizons expanded as I began offering writing classes to folks aged 55 and older, through CNU's LifeLong Learning Society.

Most of my students have been on the road of life a long time with incredible stops along the way. They are in harmony with life. Some plan to prepare family genealogical histories, or work with memoir writing; yet others yearn to create entertaining stories based loosely on actual events.

Toss topics such as weather, money, or love letters to a gathering of CNU'S LifeLong Learners, and there are as many stories as there are people in the group. A goodly number of these folks are college educated, many are retired professionals and will speak of their experiences, yet for unexplained reasons some feel ill equipped or possibly insecure about expressing themselves on paper. Is it the writing process? Is it the blank page blues?

This is a time of economic and social mobility with virtually no live-in grandmothers, grandfathers, or great aunties. Often these rich sources of family anecdotes live far, far away. My adult students tell me repeatedly that stories will be forgotten unless someone steps into the position of keeper and teller of family stories.

Who falls heir to this role? There isn't always a direct line of succession. Sometimes it is the youngest, often the family observer, who records the stories. Occasionally, it is the eldest adult child, most familiar with the passing generation, who assumes the role ("Ouch!" That shoe fits me!).

When I realized what was happening, I was a bit uncomfortable in the role of keeper of the stories. You might say the shoe pinched a bit. But oh my, as I continue the journey, I am comfortable. The shoe could fit you, too!

Although I have found among the LifeLong Learners that some would like to do family histories from a genealogical perspective, many are of the anecdotal mind set. They have stories to tell but lack confidence in two general areas: the overall writing process and converting anecdote to story. Some of the pitfalls they encounter are in organizing the material and writing in a coherent manner. The process of converting an anecdote to a story is as much of a concern as committing the story to paper.

Instead of relating family stories, some creative writers pluck a gem of wisdom, a saying, or a virtue that seems to reoccur throughout the generations, to develop. Sometimes the piece could turn out to be a "non-family related" expository work. On occasion what begins as an anecdote takes a huge curve, and facts recycled by the writer become fiction.

Session by session, I try to reassure the aspiring writers by offering writing tools, one at a time. I encourage them to keep these tools packed in readiness, for there is no telling when or in which direction the idea may beckon.

Writing tools? Relax! No need to rush out for a new computer or color printer. The tools I speak of are in this guide. My little volume offers practical tools such as ways to gather your subject matter, strategies for organizing your material, and tips for polishing your work.

But there is more. Writers need writers. Knowing that others have been there on smooth roads, up hill and down, around the corner, and sometimes forced into detour, helps. On occasion a writer plows headlong into a dead end. I smile sometimes as I think of John Bunyan's pilgrim struggling on his journey, passing through the Valley of Humiliation, Slough of Despond, and other less than scenic attractions, as part of *The Pilgrim's Progress*. Not even red shoes

1 - Reset the Compass

would have helped this fellow!

Agony and bliss are companions on every journey. For the beginning older writer it can be hair-pulling misery anticipating the writing process, until the first sentence flows into a joyous first paragraph. Now you are Mt. Vesuvius, erupting with ideas. Page after page you fill.

If you stop to read, rework, revise before you finish first draft, sometimes demoralizing thoughts like "Why am I doing this?" "Will I ever be finished?" and "Who will want to read this anyway?" erode your confidence. Relax. There is time for fine-tuning later. From other writers I have gathered thoughts and helpful examples, which may lift your spirits. Their words are sprinkled throughout this book. Consider their insights an oasis in the trek across the inevitable desert.

This book is a carefully designed guide for those who wish to express themselves, but are grappling with the problems of how to begin, how to write, and how to polish the stories. Because the strategies and techniques set forth in this book are tried and tested, and have worked for LifeLong Learners, more than likely they will work for you.

Are you ready? Now is the time to reset your compass, for collecting and writing stories will lead you in directions that you have never dreamed.

Notes

CHAPTER TWO:
The Historian's Approach

Some of you have decided to undertake the task of all tasks, writing the family history. If you are one of the lucky ones, those in generations before you left letters and diaries, possibly a complete family tree so you could easily glean documented information.

Investigating a part of the family happened rather unexpectedly to my best friend at the death of her mother. Until she died at 91, her mother guarded the secret of a weather-beaten leather trunk. At last, after a respectable length of time elapsed after her mother's death, my friend revealed to me a secret! She had access to the key—the key that would unlock the dusty old trunk, which had been tucked away under the eaves in the back of the attic, off-limits to everyone as long as her mother was alive.

On the hottest day of July, I was present in the attic for the opening of the trunk. Our imaginations worked overtime and for a moment we discussed wearing gloves but decided against it. We wondered if it would be like the opening of a Pharaoh's tomb, and by lifting the trunk lid we would be releasing all sorts of ancient viruses into the world. Would it be filled with vintage jewelry and clothing, letters from the Civil War, or turn of the century memorabilia? For all we knew it could have been Pandora's box.

The only thing the scuffed leather trunk contained besides dirt was one dusty, yellowed envelope. Tucked inside the battered envelope was a letter in pristine condition. Wondering if the letter would crumble in her hands, my friend carefully unfolded the paper. The letter was dated in 1857. Would it tell of some dark family scandal? Since it was in pre-Civil War South Carolina, perhaps the contents told of a clandestine plan! After all, there surely must have been talk of impending war.

I listened as she read the letter aloud and couldn't resist looking over my best friend's shoulder to peek at the remarkably beautiful penmanship on the pages. When she finished reading the entire letter, we looked at each other in the dim attic light. It was a two-page letter from one cousin to another complaining about not receiving any mail. The cousin writing the letter vowed it would be the last letter until a return letter was received.

Some might say, especially with the war just around the corner, that this letter, seemingly without substance, was a dead end. The mystery of why the trunk was locked and off limits for so long remains unsolved. Sitting on the floor of the dusty, stifling hot attic, my best friend and I had an epiphany as we discussed the significance of letter writing as an important means of communication for her family, and how even today her family continues to write letters. We reset the compass, and our research journey began.

The postmark on the aged envelope was from a small town in a rural area of the Piedmont region in

2 - The Historian's Approach

South Carolina. We traveled to that town and made a visit to the courthouse. We moved from office to office, from archive to archive, tracking the family, their property, and their taxes. We knew many small courthouses burned and documents were lost during the war, but we hoped our destination had been spared.

Talking to the record clerk was an experience, and worthy of a story. This particular courthouse had been burned, and some records were lost, but many were saved because town officials divided the records and hid them in various safe spots, including the old railroad stationmaster's office. Tracking a simple letter gave us not only historical data, but also geographical input and sociological commentary.

Although we had a very good time touring South Carolina as amateur sleuths, we did learn one very important research lesson from this adventure. That lesson was to remain focused. We were so excited to be on the trail and actually locate information that we consumed all details until our notebooks were a potpourri of findings, and we were on overload. The time had come for my friend to make a serious decision. Was she to do a straight family tree, finding out statistical information, such as births, marriages, deaths etc.; or would she write family stories based on the family tree?

The answer was clear. She would harvest and retell, and in some cases create new stories from her bountiful family tree. As she searched the courthouse records, less familiar family members of long ago began to come alive. It all began with a key and a letter. The challenge still remains as to how to unlock the mystery of her mother's trunk!

Where will you begin with your family history? Some researchers refer to this as the family pedigree. You could arrange the information using the traditional brackets beginning with past generations. Or

Keeper of the Stories

you could be creative. How about beginning a family tree diagram with you? You have a name, a date of birth, and a birthplace.

Try designing a reverse family tree with you as the trunk. Begin your chart by working up the trunk and branch out from there. Create two distinct branches as they branch from you, the trunk. List your parents, and add twigs, which are their birth dates, and birthplaces. Add marriage, date, place, children, dates of birth, place of birth etc. The size of the twig can connote the importance of the statistic. See how the family tree branches spread, stretching ever upward as you add more and more grandparents, great-grandparents, and relatives.

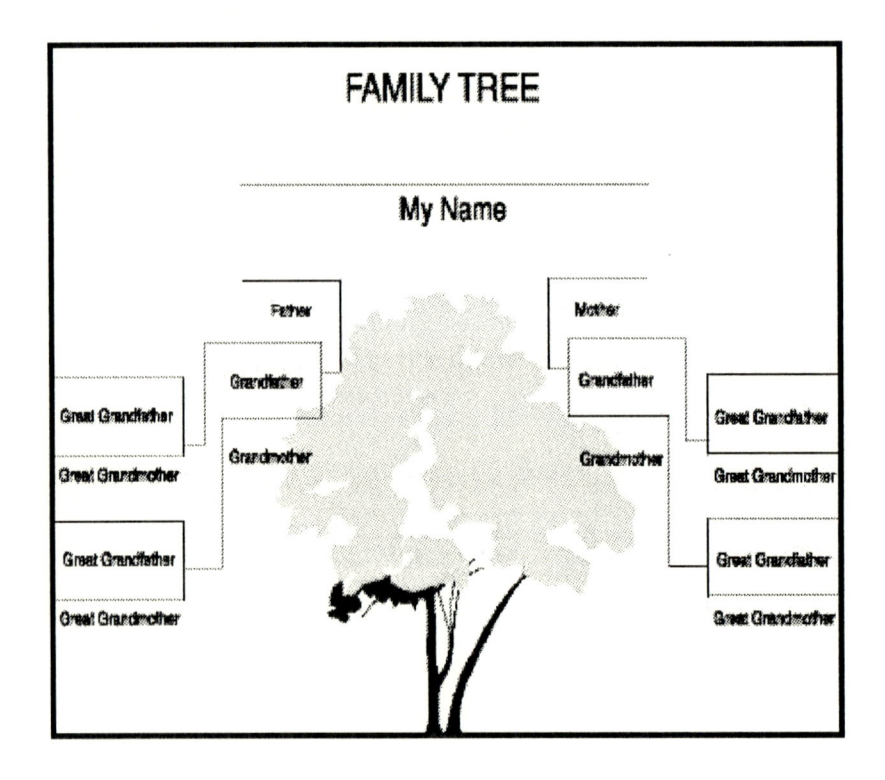

FAMILY TREE

My Name

Father — Mother
Grandfather — Grandfather
Grandmother — Grandmother
Great Grandfather — Great Grandfather
Great Grandmother — Great Grandmother
Great Grandfather — Great Grandfather
Great Grandmother — Great Grandmother

Just wait until there is the blank space. I guarantee that you will move heaven and earth to find the elu-

2 - The Historian's Approach

sive information which belongs in that space.

If you have access to a computer, visit the computer software departments at computer shops, office superstores, and other electronic specialty stores and look at the "Creating A Family Tree" programs. Assess your needs, then talk to others who have worked with the programs. It is easy as a computer beginner to get caught up with the excitement of the moment, and to spend considerable money on a program that is so sophisticated that you can't use it. Ask questions!

Researching is like being in a candy store. You have many options when gathering and recording family data. If you have a personal computer which has Internet capabilities, use it. Most local libraries have computers with access to the Internet and the World Wide Web for public to use. If you have a home computer but can't come up with satisfactory electronic search methods, don't be reluctant to go to your local research librarian for help. This ought to be fun, not exasperating. Are you timid about computers and feel as I once did, that you might get stalled on the on-ramp to the information superhighway? Here are simple ways to get your electronic search underway:

First, try a *broad search.* Type in your last name or that of a relative as a keyword and see what happens. You could be surprised. Did you ever compete in any type of event or participate in an activity, which might be covered by a newspaper or other publication? If so, your name might come up. You can narrow the search by using the last and first names as the keyword. It is downright entertaining to conduct electronic searches. The results are often mind-boggling.

There are many general search engines. *Ask Jeeves, Dogpile,* and *Google* are easy to use. Type in the name of the search engine. Then type your name in the blank that you will be offered. You may find the

Keeper of the Stories

name mentioned in connection with an article in a periodical. Others, unknown to you but with the surname you are searching, could lead (or in computer terms "link") you to a fount of information.

Another electronic alternative search method is to look up *records, on-line newspapers, and other available information sources* by typing in the name of a state or particular town and go to the links which are suggested at those websites. Often the electronic archival search saves in time and travel expense, although nothing beats the experience visiting a courthouse and reading hand-entered information in old record books.

Genealogical research is an integral part of The Church of Jesus Christ of the Latter-day Saints' beliefs. A *genealogical database* at the larger Mormon worship centers is usually available to the public. Sometimes an appointment to search their genealogical archives is necessary. It has been my experience that the folks are very helpful in assisting your search. All they ask is that if you come up with any new information or new links to information, you share your information with the Church so the new material can be added to their files. You may also write to the Mormon Family History Library:

Mormon Family History Library
Genealogical Department
35 North West Temple
Salt Lake City, UT 84150.

The Mormon Family History Library now has a web site and can be accessed at

www.Mormon.Com.

Another very helpful Mormon source is

2 - The Historian's Approach

www.familysearch.org.

After reaching this site, click on products, then go to software, PAF. You are able to download this program at no cost. Occasionally, you will come across a web page with some information, but to continue you will be charged a fee, so be alert. Not everything is free.

There are specific *websites dedicated to ancestry* that offer links to other ancestry research pages. Three very helpful sites are:

www.Ancestry.com
www.Ancestralquest.com
www.rootsweb.com

Be aware of the possibility as you visit web pages that not all the information is accurate. *Always cross-reference the information with other sources.*

Another source to tap is The *National Genealogical Society*. This organization offers research tips, source information, and helpful information for beginning researchers. The website is

www.genealogy.org/NGS.

The postal address is:

The National Genealogical Society
Educational Division
4527 Seventeenth St. North
Arlington, VA 22207-2399

For best results when writing to any organization for any type of information, keep your letter of request brief, and always include a self-addressed, stamped envelope. Every state has general as well as ethni-

17

cally specific genealogical societies. To expedite your search for these groups, check with the research librarian at your local public library.

Visiting the *local newspaper archives* in your search town should yield accurate, documented information as to what was occurring in the period that you are researching. Local events could lead to more specific information. Perhaps you find great-great grandfather organized the town's first apple festival or led the firehouse volunteers in putting out a fire in the back room of a dry goods store. These examples sound farfetched, but family historians with whom I am acquainted have found similar, curious information in their family searches.

A trip to the old neighborhood may yield information. Talking to neighbors may prove beneficial. Do your homework before you set out. If possible, have old local names you can drop as casual reference while you explain your mission. "I am the grandson of—" or, "I am the grandniece of a person who, I believe, once lived here" is a good lead and reassures suspicious folk. Although you should have questions prepared, be flexible. Ask follow-up questions. If you have an open-minded approach, you might find that an answer to one question could just open an interesting new door.

Be bold in your quest for information. People are not mind readers, so ask specific questions, carefully and tactfully. And just as carefully, record their information. You could leave a stamped, self-addressed envelope for post interview memories. Whether or not a neighborly source turns out to be a bonanza, express gratitude for the interview, and at your earliest convenience follow with a brief thank-you note. It is interesting to see how often those who are interviewed just can't "recollect" for strangers, but it is amazing how quickly something comes to mind when a prompt follow-up thank-you note arrives. Make sure your name and return address are on the envelope. You might be surprised with the correspondence.

A little appreciation goes a long way in dealing with school officials. It seems that schools have kept *"folders" on students* for as long as there have been teachers and students. Disciplinary action in response to rule infraction is a piece in the personality puzzle. Is there anything unusual about the attendance record, such as extended absences or reports of truancy? Is truancy worth a story? By all means!

When writer Jesse Stuart was a 26-year-old principal at McKell High School in Kentucky, he reveled in the coming of spring, the joy of April's greening. He recalls there came an April day when it was not in his makeup to stay within the four walls of the school, and he played hooky under the guise of hunting for truant students. Go ahead and check the school folders. I believe Stuart not only understood but also basically expected the unusually high absentee rate when he looked out the window. He claims to have written one of his favorite short stories, "Wild Plums" as a result of that day.

While I was teaching high school English, on the first day of deer hunting season many young hunters would be off with their fathers and absent from my classes. High absenteeism struck again on the first day of duck hunting season.

Would you like to know if your family member was a dedicated student with perfect attendance, or perhaps a fun-loving rascal? Do you see that little by little you can piece together a profile? Check the courses and grades. Look for teacher comments on report cards and in the student folder. What about the old junior high school or high school annual now called the yearbook? Was the relative active in sports or in any clubs? Perhaps there are senior superlatives such as most athletic, best dressed, cutest etc. Inscriptions and student comments can be revealing and lead to other names and possible sources.

Sometimes other names appear and reappear with your relative in various other venues. This is especially true in small towns. The newly discovered source may be long gone, but chances are good there are descendants. Perhaps a classmate may have also belonged to the same church. Many *small community churches* have informal historians who can offer valuable information, including a guided tour, with commentary, of the *local cemetery*. Although many old courthouses were burned during the Civil War, some historic churches were spared, so *baptism, marriage and funeral records* may be available.

"Be creative as you search," I often told my long-ago high school students as they moaned and groaned over research papers. It was their belief if there weren't a book title or an encyclopedia article to correspond with their topic, there was no information and no paper could be written. Baloney! Search, search, and search some more, by cross-referencing. Suppose you have a picture of a relative who served in the Civil War. You know nothing else. Bring your picture to a *war museum curator* or a *war historian*. You may be able to find rank, identification of medals, and unit. Probably with further research you would be able to identify troop movement, battle locations, and read casualty lists. You just might find yourself wanting to learn more, and yearning to follow one of the many Civil War trails, or to visit battlegrounds. Remember that you have reset your compass headed in the direction of fun.

Go for it!

CHAPTER THREE:
Finding Good Stories

You claim you are not a statistician, and dates are not your forte. Suppose compiling a chronologically accurate historical account of the family or your personal life worries the bejeepers out of you. The thought of dates and who begat whom distracts your from your purpose, which is writing about interesting family events, calamities, and relationships. You want the good stuff, the details. Great! But where do you begin?

James Haskett, a retired Chief Historian of the U.S. National Park Service in Yorktown, VA and member of CNU's LifeLong Learning Society, wanted to write about a branch of his family living in North Carolina from 1685 through the 1730s. That was ten or eleven generations back. Where would he begin? He did locate property and birth records. But he wanted to know what life was like for these people, so that he could provide interesting and factual information to incorporate into writing about past of his family, for his children and grandchildren.

He found four accounts of life in North Carolina, which included William Byrd's *The History of the Dividing Line*, and journals of Quaker and Protestant missionaries. It was in the accounts of the missionaries that Haskett was able to piece together housing, diet, and other salient features of day-to-day life in the region.

When he discovered that in 1672 the town of Hertford was the location for the first sermon to be preached in North Carolina, he was able to draw the conclusion that there was little if any formal religious practice in North Carolina. As Haskett explores another branch of his family, he faces the same lack of documentation—except for the peanuts factor! His theme, a thread that will carry through his research and writing, is peanuts! Because this branch comes from peanut country in Virginia, he will work with how peanuts guided the cycle of life.

One of my students struggled with the lack of information, and for her, research was difficult. When she left England after World War II, she left family behind. Today few members survive, and many factors prohibit her from returning to her homeland. Her children have grown up in America and are eager for stories. She believed she had nothing to tell, until one day in class we read Larry Woiwode's essay, "Wanting an Orange." She began to smile. As a wartime child, she was placed in a boarding school out of the city. Oranges were scarce in England, but at her school one day glorious oranges miraculously appeared on the breakfast table. Just as Haskett plans to use peanuts, she will use special foods as the thread with which to stitch her family stories.

Be of strong heart and purpose. Your stories are there. Can you remember every detail about something you said you would always remember? Probably not. Maybe you remember your first car, the color, the seat covers, or the first minor mishap. Isn't it great how time and foggy memory will help assuage that first scratch or dent! Do you remember learning to drive, your first passenger, where you went? Maybe, but chances are some things have slipped away. You could get a totally different point of view on the story or face a blank stare when asking a family member about a family related event.

One of my life stories students wanted to write about her grandfather and his wheelbarrow. Try as she might she could not get the first flicker of response from her family members. She was the keeper of the wheelbarrow and found that holding on the rough-hewn handles in the way her grandfather had so often held them put her more in touch with him. Her memories of childhood autumns, of sitting on top of a pile of leaves in the wheelbarrow, of hanging on for dear life as her grandfather wheeled her and the leaves to the pile, returned.

Weaving a good story from sketchy information is less difficult than you might suspect. Be a detective. Perseverance is key to your success. Many stories are possible simply because you are the writer.

As you challenge yourself to remember or press others to remember, be on the alert for a reoccurring fact, event, or person. It is fine to prepare a list of questions for an interview but don't anticipate anything except the knowledge that your information may take many twists and turns before it becomes a story. Instead of discussing family, you may be drawn to an event that changed the family, or a physical characteristic that plays hide and seek through the generations.

Long ago, my dad, George Maness, was a pink-cheeked, barely shaving, eighteen-year-old traveling salesman wearing a brown derby hat. He bounced around the Ohio countryside from small town to small town, sometimes by bus and eventually in an old blue coupe, to sell crochet yarn and cook pots. Early in his career he realized communication skills bordering on showmanship were crucial for his financial success. As a result, one enormous parenting focus was to constantly encourage my younger brothers and me to express our thoughts. This made for interesting and often controversial dinner conversation as we grew. Eventually we chose different vehicles for self-expression. I am a writer; my brother, Andy, is a professional musician. Marty, my second brother, is a contractor whose specialty is restoration of Victorian buildings. Terry, the third and youngest brother who didn't begin to talk until he was well over two years old, is an artist.

Today, although Dad is gone, good communication remains an important life skill for my brothers and me. From the twists and turns and interests and career choices our children are choosing, it appears that we have successfully passed along Dad's concept of the importance of communication. That aspect of our family is a story, which yearns to be written.

Take time to explore your family idiosyncrasies. If you have access to old family letters, journals or diaries, quite possibly you have hit the motherlode. Letters, diaries, and journals may address personal insights, emotions, preferences, which will provide a psychological profile, which in turn will help create the "character trait" package of your subject. Information may jump right off the page. However, there may be times when you must play detective. Now, since you have reset your compass to follow the writer's path, you at last have your first challenge. Researching a relative or episode is a puzzle, and your information may come piecemeal.

Although I am constantly challenged to find information for stories about our great Aunt Emily, I have learned a valuable lesson. I should not jump to any conclusions based on a small bit of information about this dear lady. For six months every year, she left her second floor, brownstone apartment on East 57th Street in New York City to travel "on the continent," as she referred to her European junkets. We received many letters and post cards in her ungainly scrawl. Her correspondence is a good source of information about her observations and events while traveling.

Recently, in a cookbook I inherited from my mother, I found a shopping list written in Aunt Emily's unmistakable hand. It was not a conventional list. She wrote all around the edges, on the diagonal, as well as straight across the paper . . . curious things, like checking on the price of a dress in Bloomingdale's Department Store and purchasing stamps, appended to an itemized grocery list. Seemingly unrelated things? Perhaps. However unconventional her listing process, my Aunt Emily kept lists.

I commented about the peculiar arrangement of the items on the list to a family member. My Aunt Jane said that was probably one of Emily's night lists. Night list? I had not considered that. Evidently, if Emily awakened with an item for her list, without turning on the light, she reached for the paper and pencil and wrote near the edge on one side of the paper. Then she would rotate the square of paper one turn, so if she awakened with another notation she would not write over other parts of her night list.

Seeing her unusually scrawly handwriting and peculiar listing, I was prepared to think of her as somewhat disorganized. Further research proved that was not so. This is a piece of an Emily story. As you piece together your story, keep an open mind. As I discovered, one piece does not yield an entire picture.

I found that interviewing family members greatly supplemented my information. Sometimes an aphorism, maxim, or timeworn cliché pertaining to your subject surfaces again and again. As you pick up on familiar references such as "He would give you the shirt off his back" or, "She was as wild as a March hare," you might be collecting a personality or behavior tidbit. Probe a bit deeper to find an incident which demonstrates why the reference is made. If someone tells you old Uncle So-and-So is accident-prone, probe for examples. What type of accidents? Work related or at home? Was he notoriously careless or simply in the right place at the wrong time? Maybe he was helpful, good-natured, but "all thumbs."

My dad, the consummate salesman, was known for his work ethic. When folks spoke of my dad they said his name and attributes as if they were one. "That hardworking George Maness did such and such;" or, "I saw that hardworking George Maness the other day." That work ethic flowed into our upbringing. To get us up and moving, whether to do homework, cut the grass, or some other chore, he would say the funny familiar word, "YCSSOYF," which was posted on the wall behind his desk at work. Translated, YCSSOYF means "You can't sell sitting on your fanny." In one of the last memories I have of my dad, he was standing in the kitchen with a pot of freshly brewed coffee in one hand and two mugs clinking in his other hand as he said to me, "May I sell you a cup of coffee?"

When I am together with my brothers, invariably our conversation turns to life as we knew it with our Dad. Without fail things like YCSSOYF or the ceremonial sharpening of the knife before carving the holiday roast arise. Listen carefully and take notes, for you will hear certain repeated references in relation to your subject.

Interviews are important. So whom do you interview about your subject? Formulate a master list to include descendants, former classmates, people who live in the old neighborhood. While these would seem to be good sources, they could lead to additional ones. You might take a trip to view the old neighborhood—or homeland. It is difficult to top the feedback that comes from personal contact. Telephone interviews or letters of inquiry can provide information, but should be the methods of last resort. You might decide it would be good to make notes, or to bring a small cassette recorder and tape conversations. Use whatever recording method works for you, but never trust your memory.

There is nothing worse than being unprepared for an interview. When you are all set for a great chat with someone you perceive as a font of information, and that source doesn't appear to have much to say, how can you salvage the interview? Do some homework *before* you chat. If you have a motivational tool kit from which to draw, you can stir the memory and nudge the most reluctant contact into sharing.

When you use primary sources to get information and establish the time period in which the subject of your research lived, you are into solid, accurate research. A primary source is an original record, which was made at the exact time by someone who witnessed and recorded the event. Although there are many timesaving secondary sources, these are not original documents. Historians and genealogists compile secondary sources from primary sources. It is like reading the complete newspaper article versus reading a news summary.

Why not turn to archives of the local newspaper in preparing for your interview? If possible, get photocopies made of several period front pages of the paper. Names or events may ring a bell with the aging grandson of your long ago relative. Was there a natural disaster, such as an avalanche or forest fire? A major weather event such as a blizzard, tornado, flood, hurricane, or dust storm may have occurred. War, politics, and finances are other topics guaranteed to generate conversation. Based on the old newspapers you have shared, begin with a general line of questioning and then work toward the specifics. Chatting about shared events refreshes memories. Consider the following as sample starter questions which could be generated simply by looking at various sections of the photocopied newspaper then, depending on the response, move your inquires in a specific direction:

* Let's look at the article about the drought. Did the subject's family endure the drought or another major weather event? Did they lose material goods? What did they gain? Were they forced to relocate? Were there any heroic rescues or deeds?

* Did the subject serve in the military? Did he/she enlist or get drafted? How did this affect the family? Were there promotions? Honors? War stories?

* What was the state of the national economy when you were young? Were jobs scarce or plentiful? Was there a major employer in town? What was the subject's occupation? Was the job lifelong, or did the subject change jobs? How did this affect other family members?

* Did the subject have an interest in politics? Was it an active interest, like running for office or campaigning for or against someone running for office?

* What type of entertainment came to town? Live bands, talking movies, annual summer carnivals, writers reading from their works? Were

there dances? What were some of the dance steps? What about dance tunes and jukebox music? If possible, make a tape with a variety of music from the period in question.

You have gotten all the mileage you can from the old newspapers; you've made some progress in your quest for information, but you need more.

Another simple but effective research tool is photo study. If you are fortunate, you have access to more than one photo or one type of period photo. To preserve the original photograph, make photocopies. The informal snapshots usually generate great conversation.

For many summers, we have a family gathering at the beach. For more summers than I can count, my mother-in-law brings boxes of old photographs. The conversations are lively and stories flow as the photographs are passed around the table. While some of the people remain unidentified, others are emblazoned into the family stories.

One box, referred to as the "Scotland pictures," has yielded some interesting conversation. Evidently there was a prime spot for photograph taking in the yard of a thatch roof cottage. Right at the edge of many of the photographs is some sort of shrub. Whenever the time of the photograph is in dispute or the people are in question, we look at the shrub. If the shrub is small, that means it was before So-and-so got married, or the bull gored Uncle So-and-so. But as the shrub grew, so did an entire generation of stories.

Look at the hairstyles, glasses, clothing, postures of the people, and the general composition of the picture. I have heard comments like, "That can't be Aunt So-and-so. She cut her hair. Don't you remember? She was the one who always wore an apron." Your story-gathering alarm should go off with a statement such as the hair reference, or the apron. Long ago it was rare for a woman to cut her hair. Why did she cut her hair? Was she of a rebellious nature or enduring a spell of fevers and ill health? Perhaps she was a woman ahead of her time and worked outside the home in the village. Perhaps financial reversals required work outside. There is an auntie always in an apron who never cut her hair. Why is she never without an apron? Did she cover a humble dress or her only dress? Was she a good cook? Did she leave any recipes?

And so it goes with gathering the pieces. A profile of more than one family member may emerge. Surprise! You may begin to see a pattern of family dynamics! A word of caution: do not lose your focus. A lump sum of information about several people could come your way. Take notes the best way you can during the interview, then when you are alone, rewrite and begin to organize the notes.

If you have chosen to tape record your interviews, making good follow-up notes will keep the pressure off you if something happens to the tape. Although it may seem burdensome at first, if you begin the good habit of sorting and organizing your information every step of the way, you will save time and exasperation over the long haul, if you can immediately put your finger on that interesting tidbit. You will have all the organized material and the information for quick reference on future stories.

Gathering as much concrete information as you can is important, but before you begin the formal writing process, you must gain insight into your subject to create a well-rounded profile. Prepare a personal "Think List" as you assimilate your information. Here are some suggestions to get your "Think List" started:

3 - Finding Good Stories

* *What might bring joy to your family member?*

There are intangible joys such as marriage, birth of a baby, paying off the mortgage. These hint of the significance of home and relationships. Look deeper and explore the sense of responsibility. Tangible joys could be washing a car or planting a garden. While these seem to point to joy in physical activity and love of outdoors, they could indicate a joy in a visual end result, a feeling of accomplishment for a job well done. A good cup of tea, apple pie with cheddar cheese, a fresh, fluffy towel, an aversion to wool, or refusal to pitch a recliner chair, could indicate a joy found in comfortable and familiar things. Look under that physical comfort layer, and you will discover sense of or search for security. How joy is perceived will color your conclusions.

* *People liked or disliked by your subject could be an interesting area.*

Who were the friends? Why were they friends? What drew the friends together and why did they remain friends? Was it common interests or childhood friendships? Could it have been catastrophe or shared military experiences? Now, look deeper. Do intangible attributes such as "loyal" and "nonjudgmental" describe the family member? Are these attributes reflected in other aspects of emerging profile?

* *Are there material items your family member would not give away?*

Could be of a pack rat nature, in which case, there may be memorabilia for you to view. Are there things the relative would not keep? Look beyond the immediate. Keepers might be sentimental and enjoy recalling other times, other people. That is the obvious deduction. Look under the sentimental layer and you could find the heart of a procrastinator or an indecisive person, A seemingly frugal person might save everything, never knowing when that little scrap of something may be needed. Maybe this person has had do to without and has a secret fear of being without. Does the person who refuses to become attached to material things have a sense of order which spills into other areas? Is this a no-nonsense person?

The "Think List" is another tool in your research kit. Now that you are part detective, part armchair psychologist in your search, you are ready for this startling piece of information:
Relatives may be unreliable sources.
Oh yes, they will try to recall, and they will recall as accurately as they possibly can. However, early on you need to know that every member tells a version of the overall story. Some may have personal agendas and want to get a final dig or a final bit of glorification. It is your job to sift through the various versions.

You can do it!

CHAPTER FOUR:
A Writer's Journal

How does a writer become a better writer? By writing, of course. A journal is a fun and easy way to sharpen your writing skills and explore ideas at the same time. It occurred to me that perhaps a sub-genre is emerging as more and more people turn to "journaling" for self-examination, redefining goals, and exploring new spiritual paths. For this particular writing project, I do not define journal in that mode. Innermost thoughts and personal revelations fall within my definition of a personal diary. So, is there a difference between a diary and a journal? Well, it depends on whom you ask. Perhaps it is one of those "which came first, the chicken or the egg?" circular questions. Will the earth move if you decide there are no distinct differences? Probably not.

As a writer, I keep variety of journals, and I interpret a journal as notes, comments, observations collected either in the general course of living or in concert with a project. On the other hand, a diary is usually a confidential document. Thoughts entered in a diary are personal, keep out, this means you, private property!

Perhaps it is my experience that has colored my definition, my personal distinction between a journal and a diary. On my ninth birthday, just as I entered fourth grade, my mother gave me a five-year diary. She said she believed I had reached the age when privacy and private thoughts were important. My girlhood diary was blue leather with gold-gilded pages. There was a golden clasp to be locked and unlocked with a tiny golden key. I wore my diary key around my neck on the same string with my skate key. Years later when I rediscovered my girlhood diary, I no longer had the key; however, I found that it was very simple to pick the little golden lock I once believed securely held private my heart secrets.

I used my youthful diary to discover and explore my feelings, pleasant and unpleasant. In preparation for this chapter, I have reread some of my old diaries and journals. I smiled as I read the brief entry on the day I was deemed accomplished enough by my ballet teacher that I could move from ballet slippers to pink satin toe shoes. But I certainly went at length into detail and personal agony over being teased by the older, more experienced ballerinas about having beginner bunny fur toe pads. How I wished for the wads of lambs wool the older dancers used! And oh, to have a pair of black toe shoes or white, anything but beginner's pink. Although my vocabulary was simple, my woeful words transcended the years, and for a brief moment I experienced that emotional pang which prompted the long ago entry.

As I grew, I moved from the private diary, forbidden for all eyes but mine, to a journal. Gone were the nights of recording secrets by flashlight under the covers. Dear Diary was no longer my confidante. I had a living, breathing best friend with whom I could share my deep secrets and I gave as well as received feedback on secret situations.

The journal keeping I encourage for beginning writers is basically a literary tool. As I said, I have kept a variety of journals in my lifetime; however, the one I kept while I was in college during the 1960s was filled personal revelations, social commentary, and recording my opinions of life in general. There I was in Marietta, Ohio, a picturesque small town nestled at the confluence of the Muskingum and Ohio Rivers, hand in hand with friends singing freedom songs while John Glenn was circling the earth in his small spacecraft, *Friendship 7*.

Glenn, the magnitude of his accomplishments, and my youthful self-absorption suddenly came into focus as I read a surprising notation in my journal. I met and shared a meal with John Glenn's parents. Once, while my grandfather was visiting me in Marietta, he took me to a pig roast, a fund raiser for a political candidate in Ohio. From the size of the crowd, larger than the crowd which had gathered in Marietta to hear then-presidential hopeful Richard M. Nixon speak from the steps of the armory, I came to understand that this was a huge political event. Evidently, John Glenn's parents had achieved minor celebrity status because I noted that their presence was a drawing card and many contributors' wallets opened wide. I cynically pondered for several pages in my journal to what length candidates would go to raise money for campaigns.

What can I do with a journal written through the eyes of a college student during the 1960s? Plenty! Here are the obvious uses: social commentary, an opportunity for a creative nonfiction essay, and fodder for a short story or novel. Look beyond the obvious. Each journal is a time capsule of sorts. As I prepare to write family stories, I can refer to firsthand accounts of experiences with my grandfather and other family members, written in my voice of the time.

Types and contents of journals are as varied as

the people who keep them. Some people's journals reflect a lifelong love of a subject. John James Audubon, the American bird-loving naturalist, spent much of his life traveling America's countryside capturing his observations in his journals through words and with life-size illustrations of birds in their habitats.

Another illustrator, British naturalist Edith Holden's book, *The Country Diary of an Edwardian Lady*, is a literary as well as artistic journal. Unlike Audubon's generalized journal, Holden's work involves her observations for one year, 1906, in one geographical area. She also incorporates organizational structure by examining and recording nature's events as they occur in each month of the year. She includes snippets of poetry, personal reflections, and observations, as well as a myriad of plants, animals, butterflies, and birds.

Some journals are thematic, such as the journals kept by Audubon and Holden. My daughter, Jenny, keeps a weather journal. Her entries are sporadic. She faithfully records when weather phenomena occur. She grew up in the Tidewater region of Virginia and now resides in Wilmington, NC, where hurricanes are a way of life and reporters from The Weather Channel are frequent visitors.

During an eight-year sojourn in the mountains of western North Carolina, she witnessed and wrote about the time Hurricane Hugo whirled through Boone, NC, sending Appalachian State University students scrambling to get away from windows, and ruining the university's hockey field. She also recorded the amazing events occurring during a crippling, tourist-stranding blizzard, when a local radio station was the clearing house for locating overdue people. In her journal, she kept track of folks who called in to the radio station passing messages such as turning the front porch lights on as a signal of safe haven for stranded motorists, and how the radio reported the disposable diaper air drop to a snowed-in ski resort. Then there were the tourists stranded on the Blue Ridge Parkway calling in to the station to report having to break into a school to seek shelter. She may never use this weather journal for anything except personal reflection; however, there is great material for essays or a short story should she choose to write one.

Another friend keeps a very specific weather journal. He is not a flat-out storm chaser, but he tracks lightning strikes. Of special interest to him are people who have been struck by lightning and survived. Someday he hopes to use this material for a story.

The mind does curious things during sleep. Many writers have a specific journal to record their dreams. Doris Gwaltney, a writing instructor in Christopher Newport University's LifeLong Learners program and author of *Shakespeare's Sister*, (Hampton Roads Publishing, 1996) keeps a dream journal. Although she does not chronicle every dream, she says that her dreams play an important part in generating ideas in her writing life.

She also records "day" dreams. Occasionally, she is in the middle of a big project and reaches a point where she can proceed no further, so she does her best to set aside the worrisome impasse and goes to bed. Evidently in her sleep she mulls things over and dreams some sort of solution. Frequently, when she awakens in the morning, an answer awaits her. She also uses her journal to explore and expand ideas, which later could appear as part of a larger work.

During the year that Martha Benn Macdonald collected oral histories from many senior residents of Rock Hill, SC, to include in her volume *Tea Cakes and Trolley Rides*, she kept a journal, which was separate, yet related to the project. As she came across colorful people, she did character sketches, which she might use in her poetry, fiction writing, and memoir work.

Macdonald told me of one elderly woman who gave her a handmade broom and a lot of family insight along with local history. She learned that her paternal grandmother showed the old woman, who was a young girl at the time, how to gather broom sedge, and then taught her to make brooms to sell for extra Christmas money. What Macdonald recorded in her journal are the voices of old Rock Hill, their creative spirits, and the gentle kindness of her long ago relatives. As she enters into other writing projects, especially her own family stories, she can pull interesting tidbits from her "Tea Cakes" journal.

In addition to sharpening your writing skills, another plus to keeping a journal while working on a project is as an aid in maintaining your focus. It is easy to go off on tangents as you are being bombarded with interesting information at every turn. I equate this information overload to looking in the dictionary for the spelling of a word and forgetting the word because you begin reading definitions of other words as you seek the word in question.

Establish your goal in a specific work, and do not let other good information distract you. Don't plan to remember the new items for a later project. Put the "good stuff" in your journal. By committing the new ideas to paper, you will avoid the temptation to diffuse your energies by pursuing irrelevant information; you will relieve your brain of having to process and store the information; therefore, you will keep your direction and complete the original project.

The merits of journal keeping while working on a specific writing project go beyond journal keeping as a tool for better writing, and a method by which you can maintain the focus and integrity of your work.

4 - The Writer's Journal

A journal is a great method to keep the creative juices flowing. The conventional wisdom tells writers to return time and time again to journal entries to refresh the memory about a person or an incident.

Move beyond using the journal for point of reference. The very act of writing will often shake loose whatever it is preventing you from moving along with your current project. Cartoons, movies, and television have given us classic peeks at prepared writers: the thick pad of paper, the can of sharpened pencils, the pens carefully lined up, the snack, and the totally puzzled look as they face the blank paper.

If you are experiencing "writer's block," or blank page blues as I call it, write about not being able to write. Make a list of what it is that is keeping you from writing. Write about other occasions that you or your writer friends have experienced literary dry spells. If nothing else occurs to you, draw an analogy to weather, to a long hot dry spell. How do people cope? How dry is it? Go into free fall. Indulge yourself. Enjoy the process of putting words on paper. Don't worry about sentence structure, spelling, or content. You never know what may result.

I have a friend who begins her day writing several pages of whatever is in her mind. Then she can move on to other projects. I can't do that. I feel as though I am a blank, a clean slate, and I indulge myself, immerse myself in the sights and sounds of morning. I jot things down before I sleep. Therefore, I don't challenge my brain to remember things through the night. Otherwise it is a clock-watching night because I haven't given my brain permission to relax.

It is my experience as a writer that when I am struck by an idea, my journal is not always with me, so I write on whatever is close at hand. As I was driving home from work recently, I was listening to news on the car radio. From a larger news story, out jumped an ear-catching phrase. With a small pencil stub on a paper napkin, I wrote, "fire in progress." Instead of faithfully recording the phrase in my journal when I got home, I taped the paper napkin onto a page. Will I ever come back to that phrase? Probably. I have done it before. Bear Wallow Road, a street name which about caused me to put my car in a ditch nearly three years ago as I passed the street sign, is an important road name in my second novel now in progress. Today I heard a lilting piece of music for violin and piano, *The Village Wedding*. And so it goes.

You can keep a journal. All you need is paper and pencil. As a youthful journal keeper, I often studied family photos of our white clad Victorian aunties lounging ever so gracefully on large front porches. I could easily have been one of those Victorian gentlewomen resting gracefully in a wicker chair on a large front porch writing in a floral fabric bound journal. Of course the glass of lemonade garnished with a whole strawberry, an orange slice, and mint leaf would be on the stand beside me.

Although I never went so far as to achieve the Victorian look, I did try to keep a journal in a lovely Italian blank-page, hardbound book, but I got frustrated because I couldn't move and reorganize the order of the pages or the order of the entries. I reclaim from my kids their castoff, loose-leaf, three-ring binders. In order to personalize a binder, first I cover it with a collage of fabric or varieties of elegant wrapping paper, and then I seal the surfaces with clear acrylic spray. Now I can arrange and rearrange to my heart's desire.

It is important to me for future reference to date all journal entries. It is also helpful to designate the location, even if the idea strikes on the interstate or in the grocery store parking lot. Because of the versatility of the loose-leaf binders, I find there are times that I sort of cross-pollinate my journals and rearrange entries by topic, person or event. Consider the possibilities of a humorous essay based on thoughts gathered in a grocery store parking lot. There may come a time I wish to return the page to its primary spot in the original journal. I can do that merely by looking at the date.

I paste things, highlight items, write in margins and appear to create general havoc in my journals. To recycle my paper supply, which constantly dwindles, I make a big X on the written side of scratch copies and use the clean side for my journal entries. I can do this because I use a ring binder.

Because I am a tactile person, I enjoy paper and the ritual of sorting and arranging. Journal keeping is simple if you have access to a computer. You can cut and paste and delete to your heart's content. But even in the wonderful world of computers, things can go amiss. Spare yourself unnecessary agony. Always keep a paper copy and an updated backup disc of your electronic journal just in case your computer crashes.

I have often wondered what the comments would be if my eclectic journals were available to others. It seems I have kindred spirits in this world who have shed themselves of the conventional journal-keeping mystique. Dan Eldon, a young photojournalist, had many accomplishments and adventures in his brief life, including leading a relief mission in Africa. Eldon tops my list of maverick journal keepers.

In 1993 when Dan was just 22 years old, he was stoned to death in Somalia while covering the civil war there for Reuters News Agency. However, Dan left behind a series of incredibly colorful journals from which his mother, Kathy Eldon, serving as editor, compiled *The Journey is the Destination: The Journals of Dan Eldon* (Chronicle Books, 1997). His journals are a collage of writings, photos, labels, and an official document pasted here and there. Sometimes he wrote using photographs as his paper, painted borders on new pictures, commented on old pictures, and in general filled the pages with his life and his energy.

So now it is your turn. If you haven't started a writer's journal, why not begin today? You can do it. The only rules are your rules.

Notes

CHAPTER FIVE:
The Experience of Others

At the drop of a hat, Sheila Kay Adams, a lifelong resident of Madison County, NC, will recount childhood memories of front porch sitting, hearing stories and learning ballads from her "Granny," great-aunt Dellie Chandler Norton, a well-known balladeer. Originally a teacher, Adams felt the call to perform, so she left the classroom to sing ballads, tell the old stories, and in general share her mountain heritage. Eventually she had collected enough material to make several commercial tapes of the old ballads and stories. Also, she wrote a book, *Come Go Home With Me* (University of North Carolina Press, 1995) in which she captured the essence of growing up in Sodom, a small, rather isolated mountain town which has since disappeared.

Seriously gathering the old stories is different from casual porch sitting, enjoying the stories, and hoping to recall them later. Adams recommends acquiring a voice-activated tape recorder and going directly to the best sources: parents, grandparents, aunts, uncles, cousins, etc. She offers the following helpful advice:

> Be prepared for long afternoons of what might appear, at first, to be rambling, unconnected conversations that aren't going where you'd hoped. Then go back and really listen to what you have. . . . You'll be delighted with what you hear . . . turns of phrases, pronunciation of words, events that touch your heart, make you laugh, or bring tears to your eyes. And when you write, write about what you know, what you hear, the way they said it, and not just the words they said. Make it real for you. Then, I promise, it'll be real for other folks too.

Over the years I have been in and out of the classroom teaching various literature, language arts, and writing courses. In 1968 I was living in Yorktown, VA, married with one child, and in my first year of teaching (or, possibly, administering) high school English to less than motivated students. On some really dark and grueling days, my mother cheered me by updating me on the innovative ideas of another first year English teacher. She told me that the greenhorn teacher, stepbrother to the young woman who lived across the street from my family home in Wheeling, WV, was teaching in a rural place in the north Georgia mountains called Rabun Gap. He made a phenomenal breakthrough with his less than motivated students. He took time to listen, carefully listen, to his students, broke from the traditional methods, and as a result *Foxfire*, a magazine created and written by his students, was born. The teacher's name was Eliot Wigginton.

Evidently Wigginton, even as a young, beginning teacher, realized the wealth of traditional stories passed by word of mouth from generation to generation not only in the Appalachian Mountains but everywhere, would disappear as the eldest generation departs this life if these stories were not committed to paper. The plan was for his students to talk to their grandparents. In the course of it all, it would seem his students benefited in many ways. How could they not help but develop pride when they learned of their heritage? I am sure another plus to the project was intergenerational communication. It seems that "old timers" often twinkle when given the opportunity to celebrate and share with the younger generation the things they enjoy.

The project took off, and soon so much quality material had been produced that the students, with the help of Wigginton, compiled the first in a long series of *Foxfire* books. One session with any of the *Foxfire* books will help readers get a peek into the past, and come to understand that the young people in Wigginton's English classes collected the stories, photographed crafts, and related lifestyles in a way that would rival any university researcher.

Nikki Giovanni, a prolific poet and writer, is Professor of English at Virginia Polytechnic Institute and State University, better known as Virginia Tech, in Blacksburg, VA. During a conversation with me, she shared her awe and respect for our older citizens; she helped me understand that rich history will be lost as the older citizens pass from this earth. She said to me, "It is important for seniors to write . . . write about themselves. Look at what we can learn from what they have seen! There is a world to talk about."

I was involved with teaching older beginning writers, and I was keenly interested in Giovanni's involvement with older writers. She knows this subject well, for she spends time at Warm Hearth Retirement Community as a facilitator for their writing workshop. Giovanni and Cathee Dennison compiled and edited the work of the 80-90 year old writers into a volume,

Appalachian Elders—A Warm Hearth Sampler (Pocahontas Press, 1991). Her interest in older writers and their stories remains keen.

To pay tribute to grandmothers, whom she considers the keepers of our traditions, Giovanni contacted friends for poems, stories and recollections about grandmothers. She also tapped into a marvelous source, ninety-year-old writers. She compiled and edited *Grand Mothers: Poems, Reminiscences, and Short Stories About The Keepers Of Our Traditions* (Henry Holt and Company, Inc., 1996). Did she overlook grandfathers? Certainly not. *Grand Fathers: Reminiscences, Poems, Recipes, and Photos Of The Keepers Of The Traditions* (Henry Holt and Company, Inc., 1999) emerges as the touching companion piece for the successful *Grand Mothers*.

Little did Martha Benn Macdonald, former English instructor at the College of William and Mary, Williamsburg, VA, realize when she returned to her childhood home of Rock Hill, SC, that she would take on a writing project based on colorful stories of her hometown. When she arrived in Rock Hill to care for her aging mother, she took the position of Director of the Retired Senior Volunteer Program. Between extensive conversations with her mother and her affiliation with and access to rich resources, the older townsfolk, she became aware of how many landmarks and vintage people were fading from the scene in the old town. She also began to have a sense of her roots, her heritage, as she interviewed the older residents. Their information was a great resource because there were no official historical accounts written of the town for her to consult.

In creating *Tea Cakes and Trolley Rides*, (Lenoir Printing, 1995) she did not select a socio-economic-based historical commentary in recounting life in a small southern town. She employed the premise of a fictional narrator escorting children on a walking tour, to weave the collected stories into a gentle, eclectic history of Rock Hill. In this literary narrative she preserves the voices of the old mill workers, former slaves, railroad workers, and doctors' families as well as the way of life in the old mill town. There are stories of doctoring and home remedies, chamber pots and the first home to have self-styled indoor running water. There are traditions such as an annual party for twins, sweeping the yards and whitewashing the trees. There were interesting events which shaped the town, such as the manufacture of 7,000 Anderson Automobiles from 1915-1925 and the reopening of the old tobacco factory as a combination apartment, grocery and dance hall before it was finally destroyed by fire.

Just as stories fade and the people pass on, so do memories of the buildings. *Tea Cakes and Trolley Rides* also contains many original pen and ink sketches rendered by local artists. The drawings are of local historic churches, commercial buildings and homes. Because Macdonald believes that the history of the buildings and the memories of activities within the buildings will fade once they are gone, she thought it was important to have these illustrations as well as stories.

Leaving Pipe Shop (Scribner, 1997) is an engrossing memoir by Deborah E. McDowell, a professor of English at the University of Virginia in Charlottesville, VA. Not only does she write of family, but she also offers a social commentary of growing up as a child of color in Bessemer, AL, just as the winds of change were sweeping the economic as well as political Southern landscape.

Evidently she had no plans for memoir writing when she returned to her childhood home. After some not so subtle family pressure, she began the project.

She writes in a clear, gently objective voice often tempered with subtle humor. Each chapter relates a milestone in family history. As McDowell draws you into her world, she offers varied levels of meaning. For example, the chapter entitled "Pecans" would appear at first reading to be her childhood memories of cousins and Christmas, but in taking on a deeper level, McDowell offers her readers a poignant study of her mother and her family's complex and touching relationship.

The Easter of fine hairdos but no new outfits is described in the chapter titled "Easter Sunday." In this section McDowell details a local visit of the Rev. Martin Luther King, Jr, the boycott of Birmingham AL, merchants, and the strong sentiment shown towards the poor soul who ignored the boycott to retrieve her new garment from layaway in a department store. "Records" is the final chapter in *Leaving Pipe Shop*. Once again, she subtly moves her readers to a deeper, more intimate portrait of life. All who have tried to fill in the pieces in the puzzle of family history will be able to relate to McDowell's search for information about her father's death. In her quest for information, she manages to unearth more questions than answers.

It is good to discuss how professional writers work with ideas, but sometimes it is equally important to see how regular people, nonprofessional writers, develop ideas and write stories. Many of my students are more comfortable with their own writing if they can see how other real students tackle writing assignments. Some of my students have graciously granted me permission to use their work as samples in this chapter and other chapters.

Elsie Duval and Robert Kelly are members of Christopher Newport University's LLS. Each enjoys writing stories which revolve around personal anecdotes and observations, but as you will see, each approaches from a different prospective.

Duval, a lifelong resident of Newport News, VA, has been a member of LLS for many years. In 1998 one of her articles was published in *Reminisce*, a popular magazine of reflection and recollection. Her essays not only reflect personal experience, but also offer a lighthearted social commentary. In "About Corsages" she discusses the significant role corsages played in the social lives of young girls who lived and loved in the 1930s.

Notice the progression of the piece. Right away she indicates it is not in present day. She reveals the significance of wearing or not wearing a corsage on Easter Sunday in the 1930s. In the body of the piece, she moves from general to specific by detailing an occasion of her personal corsage dilemma. She comes full circle to a conclusion about present day dearth of corsages.

ABOUT CORSAGES
by
Elsie Duval

Back in the 1930s when I was somewhere between twelve and twenty, a florist corsage played a particular role in romantic relationships. It was most important for me not to miss church on Easter Sunday, since that was the day when a casual "corsage census" would determine WHO was going with WHOM. When potential lovers were spotted sitting with her family in the third pew from the front, wedding rumors were sure to follow. If any girl wearing a corsage arrived alone, there was considerable speculation as to whether it had been John, or maybe Jack, who sent her yellow roses this year. Other young ladies, whose garments were unadorned, might be promptly judged as either "available" or otherwise "undesirable." Few escaped rigid scrutiny.

In those long ago college years, most couples did not go steady, and in fact the most popular girls dated students from several different universities. Naturally, some of them received more than one Easter corsage, and a problem often developed around what to do with the spares. Knowing that even the most beautiful blooms would be dead by Tuesday, some smart girls like me began to negotiate early for permission to wear some such leftover to church on Easter Sunday. It was what is now perceived as a win-win situation, yet it was necessary to accept the risk of conjecture surrounding the probability of producing an anonymous new beau.

Throughout those decades, it was understood that certain major events demanded that all male guests send flowers. No exceptions permitted. One such happening at Agnes Scott College was the Junior-Senior Banquet, which we regarded as the social highlight of any year. Invariably, students issued invitations to the most important men in their lives at that particular moment, and as an innocent bystander, I devised my own way of distinguishing between girls who had something good going and those who didn't. After the ball was over, it became clear who had an unexciting blind date, and who was enjoying a hot romance, because I realized that passionate hugging and kissing means certain death to a corsage. Careful examination for clues, on the other hand, could prove rather embarrassing to those whose relationships were plainly platonic. In fact a casual friendship was the base from which my own date was selected. With moonlight and music, the evening was filled with magic and proved memorable indeed. Still, for obvious reasons, the next morning my lovely corsage still looked fresh enough for a second time around. Not so with others. On sudden impulse, I stomped those blossoms to death right on the spot, and I walked away smiling indulgently at the mangled mass left under foot.

I glanced around St. Andrew's Episcopal Church last Easter Sunday just to see how many women were wearing corsages in the 1990s. After a quick head count, I concluded that today's florists must make their living by selling potted plants. In spite of it all, there was one precious 90-year-old widow sprinting down the aisle with a white orchid pinned to her purse. I felt sure this was one girl who never ever once in her lifetime would have stomped a corsage to death.

Robert Kelly grew up in and around Tacoma,

WA; therefore, many of his family stories are flavored with his northwestern heritage. It is his plan to leave for his grandchildren a chronicle of a lifestyle that is rapidly passing. And so in his lighthearted essay, "Thunder in the Basement," Kelly mixes family foibles with interesting if not curious facts about lifestyle in the northwestern United States in a less sophisticated but creative and innovative time.

Notice how Kelly begins with a general profile of Tacoma, WA. As he builds his story, Kelly uses sawdust, a by-product of the lumber industry, as a transition to a specific topic, his father and his father's desire to save money. As Kelly builds suspense, he also subtly, perhaps inadvertently, reveals his character, his sense of responsibility, and his practical nature which seem to be a direct contrast to his father.

THUNDER IN THE BASEMENT
by
Robert Kelly

I grew up in Tacoma, Washington. Tacoma was the lumber capital of the world in the early 1900s having more sawmills and producing more finished lumber than any other place in the universe. Forests of Douglas fir that surrounded the city stretched into the Cascade Mountains. Sawmills lined Tacoma's waterfront, and ships moored at their piers to load and carry lumber to the ends of the earth. Lumber was king and that influenced my life in many ways.

A good influence was a high level of cultural activity. We had beautiful parks, a good museum, a symphony orchestra, and an excellent concert series. I remember hearing Rachmaninoff play the piano when I was thirteen.

One of the unwanted by-products of the lumber industry influenced my life in a peculiar way. That was sawdust. Great mountains of sawdust towered one hundred to two hundred feet into the air around the sawmills. True, there were burners to dispose of sawdust, but it was produced faster than it could be burned. So it piled up, unwanted and unloved.

When I was five or six, someone had a brilliant idea of heating homes with sawdust. A sawdust-burning furnace was developed and became an instant success. People left coal, wood, and electricity behind and bought sawdust-burning furnaces as fast as they could be manufactured. Daddy was one of those people. Because Tacoma had one of the lowest electric rates in the country, our house was heated with electricity. A simple flick of the switch made our house warm as toast. But Daddy was going to beat the cost of electricity with sawdust. Men came out to our house and put a great furnace in the middle of our basement and walled off a larger area for sawdust storage.

Daddy missed one point. At the sawmill, sawdust was moved to the great piles by conveyor belts. When our first load of sawdust arrived, it was dumped in the garage driveway. That was thirty feet and one story away from the sawdust storage area in the basement. Daddy called the sawdust dealer to ask why he had not unloaded it by conveyor belt through the two basement windows into the storage area. The dealer explained that sawdust was dumped, period.

That sawdust, somehow, would have to be moved into the garage then down a flight of stairs into the basement area that Mother used for her washing machine, and then into its storage area. Dad's major in Classics at college brought him a Rhodes Scholarship but wasn't much help in preplanning how to get sawdust moved from the driveway to its storage area.

Making light of this quandary, Dad remarked to Mother that at age thirty-six he needed exercise and this was a God-sent opportunity. Picking up a shovel, he began to move the sawdust into the garage, then down the stairs after moving Mother's washing machine to a safe place and removing cans from his car. He filled these cans with sawdust and dumped them into the conical sawdust hopper that fed the furnace. He took a couple of newspapers, stuffed them into the furnace and lit them. The sawdust took fire, and we were in business!

To save more of the electric bill, Daddy had a hot water coil put in the furnace. It was connected to the hot water tank and was to produce free hot water when the furnace was in use. This arrangement, however, had an unforeseen drawback. In the cold of winter, when the furnace burned full

5 - The Experience of Others

blast all day, it boiled the water in the heating coils. This boiling produced a low grumble in the basement as the steam from the heating coils bubbled into the hot water tank. When this occurred, Mother or one of us would go down in the basement and open the hot water faucets in the double laundry tubs and let them run. This drew off the hot water allowing the cooler supply water fill the tank.

This worked fine until a particular, cold winter afternoon that I remember. When I arrived home from high school, the house was locked. Apparently, Mother was still at her bridge club. As I unlocked the back door, I could hear the tank rumbling in the basement. When I opened the door, the rumble turned to thunder in the basement. The house was hot as an oven. The furnace must have been left on high. I turned right around and went back out on the porch closing the door behind me for protection. Fear gripped me as I realized that not only was the water in the heating coils boiling, the entire hot water tank was boiling. Then I thought of how important our house was to us, and all the things in it.

In panic I reentered the kitchen and raced for the basement door. When I opened the door, I knew the tank sounded as if it were ready to blow up. I could visualize the tank jumping up and down on its stand as the water boiled and gurgled inside making enough steam to blow me and the house to kingdom come.

Sensing the end was near, I ran down the basement steps and right by the rattling and thumping tank to the laundry tubs. I opened both hot water faucets and bolted to the safety of the garage. Steam hissed out of the faucets like wild banshees chasing their victims. I watched as the steam poured into the garage, and I could see beetles, earwigs, and spiders running for their lives. I threw open the garage doors, and steam poured into the neighborhood.

As cooler water entered the tank, it quieted down and was finally silent. I turned off the faucets and went upstairs and opened both the front and back doors to clear the steam from the house. Then, I closed the damper on the furnace.

Mother arrived a few minutes later wondering why the outside doors were open in midwinter and why I was sitting on the living room davenport eating a bowl of vanilla ice cream covered in chocolate sauce.

CHAPTER SIX:
Taming Wild Thoughts

Something happens to catch the writer's interest. Perhaps an event, a phrase, or a sound rekindles the memory fire, and with no particular plan you make a private promise to really get it down on paper this time. Ideas are popcorn exploding everywhere, but it seems like an impossible task to tame those mini explosions and wild thoughts into workable material. Gloomy thoughts come, and motivation wanes before the first word is committed to paper.

When I discussed organizing story information with my LifeLong Learners, they smiled politely. "Yes," they said, "we might as well get into that."

First I heard the collective sigh. Then I heard the timeless question that every teacher from middle school on up hears: "Does this mean we HAVE to do outlines?"

Someone else piped up, "Oh no, not one of those for every 'A' there is a 'B' things!"

While outlining is an integral part of organizing the material, it is just one of four steps I recommend in the organization process. The other organizational helpers are form, structure, and time.

Form is the appearance of the work. It is what the writer's audience notices initially. Not to be confused with whether the manuscript is single or double-spaced, or whether the pages are numbered at the top or the bottom, form is reflected in a catchy title or an interesting first sentence. More than likely, titles such as "The Tale of Old Blood and Guts Bill," or "In Grandma's Garden" give the reader hints at the nature of the story.

In a concrete way, compare form to the seemingly unsinkable British steamer, *Titanic*. Recall her beauty and how she was deemed unsinkable. *Titanic* in her time was a magnificent vessel cutting through the waves on her maiden voyage to America. In her elegant beauty, the ship hints of wonderful music, fine dining, and lavish rides. Form will hint to the reader as to the direction the piece is headed.

Form cannot stand alone in organizing the material. Structure is the skeleton of the work. It is the way the piece is organized. Without structure the writer's labor of love is weak and confusing and will not take the reader on a pleasant journey. Consider once again the image of *Titanic*. During the trans-Atlantic voyage, she struck an iceberg and went down in less than three hours. *Titanic* was a beautiful, seemingly ocean-worthy craft, but she lacked structural integrity to withstand a collision with an iceberg, and she sank.

Structure is the way the piece is organized. For the purpose of discussing memoir writing, reflective pieces, or creative nonfiction, the structure in these works might be a straightforward narrative in story format, or it might be an essay. The work could be a biography, a life from birth to death and all the happenings in between. If the events are not presented in some logical way, the reader may become confused, the writer has missed the point; therefore, the integrity of the piece has been compromised and will surely sink in the reader's eyes just as if it were the *Titanic*.

Remember this: if a series of events is presented in a jumbled way, there is no sense of rising momentum leading to the moment, the epiphany, and the insight intended by the author. Structure validates and supports the promise of the title and first sentence.

Time is another structural device that aids in taming the wild thoughts and creating a readable story. The writer may choose the chronological approach. In using this approach, the writer has many options on the order in which events are presented. Take the example of a woman is who has just delivered a healthy baby. The writer may adjust the order of events to track back to the new mother's courtship and marriage. Although the reader knows the outcome is a bouncing baby, the writer's job may be to reveal the events which led up to the blessed birth.

Another popular method to control time is by historical chronology. The writer faithfully keeps the order of events as they actually occurred in real life. The larger job is to engage and entertain the reader with a series of episodes that build increasing interest on the way to the big finish.

Keeping with the idea of a series of episodes, and to make the concept of managing time a little less difficult, construct a timeline. You don't have to use a chronology of birth to death. Pick a significant event and break it into mini-events. The timeline does not have to be elaborate, so don't spend your creative energy drawing the perfect straight line. This horizontal line indicates ordinary day-to-day life. Above the line is positive territory and below is negative territory. This sounds like stock market talk, and perhaps life's ups and downs are as fickle as the stock market.

Here is a classic writing scenario when the

timeline can be invaluable. Finally, you have gathered story ideas, your interviews are completed, you have searched last of the records and documents, and you have a pile, stacks, and perhaps even boxes of information. Now it seems as if the mountain of "good stuff" is too steep to climb. The project is out of control. There are tidbits of information on file cards, loose papers, in folders and tablets, and your focus is buried somewhere in the mound.

Take heart! It is possible to organize thoughts and materials concurrently, thus easily reclaiming the focus of the project. Look for important events: the birth of a child, college graduation, trips, and promotions are positive examples; illness, death, financial loss, or other disappointments are negatives. Has there been a strategic move or job change? A timeline can be designed for an entire family, for a specific family member, or for a specific event.

An example of a specific event, which brings out the best and the worst in me, is the annual gathering of the women on my husband's side of the family to prepare the traditional holiday plum pudding. Weddings, funerals, and family holidays, school picnics, or work-related reunions are classic events that are fertile ground for both positive and negative dynamics. If the stories in this project relate specifically to one person, push the mound of collected information aside and make a timeline for that person. Begin with birth and end with death (if the subject is deceased).

As you draw a horizontal line, think of your timeline as a ruler. Where the inches are marked could represent significant events. In measuring time, use the horizontal line as a base and draw an arrow pointing up to the high points or down from the line to indicate low points. It would be easy to accentuate either positive or negative, but you should remain

6 - Taming Wild Thoughts

objective. General high points are education, love, marriage, and children. Low points are illness, job loss, and destructive, natural catastrophes like fire, flood or blizzard. There are also the in-betweens such as vacations and geographical relocations. You might find that constructing a timeline yields fresh story ideas and insight into behavior patterns as well as being a sound organizational exercise.

Materials, data, and stories you have collected provide rich detail and supportive information, but if you suffer from "where is that gosh darn paper with such-and-such on it! I know I put it someplace in this pile!" syndrome, then you have experienced the loss of precious creative time and energy shuffling papers. It is possible to lose data on the computer, too. Perhaps you have saved some information in a file, but can't remember which file. That shouldn't be a problem, if you have printed the information. It is a nightmare sorting through computer printouts, tough, if they were not filed as they were printed.

Some people prefer the box and index cards filing procedure. However, the loose-leaf notebook with dividers is a quick, easy-to-read reference tool. You will need a big three ring, loose-leaf notebook with dividers, plenty of paper, scissors, hole punch, and paper glue. Label a section for each significant area, and as you come across information pertaining to that topic, put it in the notebook. Glue note cards to the notebook paper if necessary.

How about all those photocopies of pictures, newspaper articles, and legal documents you have made? Use the hole punch! File your materials in each appropriate section. If you are puzzling over the event while writing it, you can turn to the germane section your resource notebook. You have interviews, anecdotes, hastily written story ideas and other information together to peruse as you firm your focus. All

61

this may seem unnecessary, if you work on a computer. Do keep in mind that without warning catastrophes can occur in the computer files. Even when you have a backup file, sometimes a portion of the work or the entire project can be lost. If you have printed the copy from your files, that is good, but you still need to keep the printed material in an organized manner.

Consider this: you may be on vacation, the computer is at home, and yet you want to work on your project. An organized notebook tucked in your bag is all the resource you need for writing as you sit by the fire in a snowy mountain cabin or on the beach watching the morning sun rising as a red dot on the horizon.

A chronological timeline does not always work. You might choose a thematic approach rather than moving from birth to death. Eleanor Hill, one of my students, writes humorous, sometimes touching, stories based on growing up with prankster brothers. In organizing her collection she could, rather than spotlighting the life and times of a certain person, create a thematic line based on the escalation of quantity and quality of the practical jokes. Perhaps there was the culmination, the prank of all pranks, that vaulted her brothers towards more mature behavior, possibly divided the family loyalties forever, or even exalted her to innocent princess status.

If the project encompasses a collection for an entire family, taming wild thoughts is still possible. It might take more than one notebook. The individuals in the family may have their own timelines as an offshoot of the major family line. The notebook is an invaluable tool here, too. Each notebook could be dedicated to a century, or a decade. In each notebook, have a timeline pertaining to each branch of the family, each subject, or each time frame. Separate categorized materials by dividers. Color tabs are another way for quick reference. Assign each family member a color tab. Tab each section relating directly to that person. Assign color tabs to the crossovers that invariably hop from story to story. Add as many tabs to a section as is necessary. All this seems like lots of sorting and arranging busy work, but in the end it will save you so much time and keep the frustration level way down. The timeline notebook may turn out to be a unique legacy for your personal history.

Now you need to move to phase two in taming your wild thoughts. Whether you refer to the process as brainstorming, or hear others call the process mind mapping or webbing, don't let terminology slow you. Mind mapping is a jazzy new term for free association of thoughts. Remember the old days in high school English class when the teacher had you brainstorm an idea as a prewriting exercise before she assigned the paper or essay? If you have brainstormed, you have used the mind mapping technique.

How do you prioritize and keep all that brilliant organization in your head? You don't. You create an idea paper. You put your main idea in the center of the paper and then in each corner write whatever you think relates to the main idea. Add smaller, supporting details to the big ideas.

Keep in mind all things should relate the main idea in the center of the paper. Sometimes it looks like disorganized doodling as you group like ideas together, but as you play with the ideas, you are gradually getting organized. A clustering diagram I play with resembles a sunburst. The main idea is in the face of the sun. All the rays of the sun are the "bright" ideas. What shape your clustering diagram takes is of little importance to your completed story. Seeing the ideas, organizing them, and evaluating their degree of importance to your story is what matters.

Clustering Diagram for "Tea Time -- Aunt Emily's Way"

Tea Tray
Afternoon
Setting the Tray
Cups and Saucers
Tea Time
Morning
Sugar and Creme
TEA TIME Aunt Emily's Way
Love of Tea
Tea Making Process
Serve
Heat Water
Strain
Steep
Add Tea
Prepare the Pot

Note that although this mind-mapping pattern resembles a sunburst, your ideas may take on any or all sorts of shapes, depending on the progress of your brainstorming session.

In writing about her prankster brothers, Eleanor Hill could place the general category, "Practical Jokes," in the center and each bright idea could be one trick. Springing from the trick could be those involved, the innocent and the guilty, but location, motivation, severity, repercussions, and punishments as a result of the prank, must also be included.

Clustering or webbing is an effective tool for organizing ideas within a single story as well as ordering a collection. As I mentioned in Chapter One, I set about to write Aunt Emily stories because I planned to give my daughter Jenifer Emily a teapot that belonged to my mother's Aunt Emily. I wanted to write a story to enhance the symbolic value of a gift, but I didn't want to get into our Victorian auntie's life from start to finish. As a gift to accompany the teapot, I wrote about the daily teatime ritual, which was one of her defining characteristics.

I chose the broad topic of "Tea Time - Aunt Emily's Way." There are five major points "radiating" from the central bright idea. The major categories include the time of day tea was drunk, tea-drinking companions, the type of tea used, how the tea was made, and what items were on the tea tray. Smaller supporting ideas flare from the major points.

For some lucky writers, an organization plan forms during the clustering process. Sometimes the story can be written without further planning. Free-spirited writers sigh in the chains of outlines while others find security in the outlining process.

An outline does not have to be a head-scratching bugaboo. It can be as simple as jotting down the major points you want to make in the order in which you wish to make them. I could do that by referring to my clustering diagram for my tea story. A possible sequence begins with Aunt Emily's love of tea, the type of tea, contents of the tea tray, the actual tea

Keeper of the Stories

making process, and frequency of tea drinking.

Do you remember your high school research paper and the required outline as LifeLong Learners do? My memory is of the topic outline. I can hear my teachers now. "Remember, for every I there is a II; for every A there is a B." And on it went. Formal is the best description of a topic outline. This is a simple-to-reference, yet detailed organizational method. Once again, the cluster earns its way. Perhaps you have more details than should be included in this particular story. By using the topic outline, you can remain focused on the main ideas. Remember to keep the cluster because some little add-on from the brainstorming could be a major point in a story yet to be developed.

The official order for the topic outline is as follows: Use Roman numerals to number the main topics. Set off the subheadings with capital letters and the supporting material with Arabic numbers. If you find it necessary to include more supporting ideas, use lower-case a, b, and c. Don't forget! The English teacher was right about parallel ideas. For every I there really must be a II and so on. As you set up the topic outline, remember to indent. If you are typing use five spaces. Use good spacing judgment if you are writing in longhand. I have chosen "Tea Time - Aunt Emily's Way" for the sample topic outline:

I. Love of Tea
    A. Tea Time
        1. Morning
            a. grapefruit
            b. paper
        2. Afternoon
            a. sandwiches
            b. sweets
            c. guests for tea
    B. Tea Tray

            1. The tray
                a. cups
                b. sugar
                    (1) granulated
                    (2) cubes
                c. cream
                d. demitasse spoons
            2. The teapot
                a. cozy
                b. strainer

II Tea Making Ritual
        A. Prepare the pot
            1. Heat water
            2. Warm pot
        B. Add tea leaves
            1. Steep
            2. Strain
            3. Serve

III Aunt Emily's Visit
        A. To meet namesake
        B. Cambric Tea
            1. Milk
            2. Sugar
        C. The Gift
            1. The teapot
            2. The spoon

Another type of outline is the sentence outline. This form is exactly as it sounds. This is not a one or two word topic outline, but an outline written in complete sentences. In the beginning this appears to be a lot of work. If you do use a sentence outline, you will see your story begins to take shape. As you work on your writing project, you will select your most important ideas and embellish them. The beauty of the sentence outline is that you will see that core ideas of the story are expressed in more detail than one or two words of a topical outline. The sentences are right there for you. It will be clear to you what you had in mind when you created the sentence outline.

I Aunt Emily enjoyed a good pot of tea.
    A. There were two times each day she drank tea.
        1. She made her first pot of tea for breakfast.
            a. She prepared grapefruit to have with her morning tea.
            b. She read the morning paper as she drank her tea.
        2. She prepared the second pot of tea in the afternoon.
            a. She served egg, chicken, or tuna salad finger sandwiches.
            b. She offered sweet treats such as sugar cookies and stuffed dates.
            c. Often friends were invited for afternoon tea.
    B. Morning and afternoon tea trays were set in similar ways.
        1. A plain tray was for daily use and an ornate silver tray for Sunday.
        2. Cups and saucers were placed on the tray.
        3. The sugar bowl was filled with either granulated sugar or cubes.
        4. Beside the sugar was a cream pitcher.
        5. There was also a plate of lemon slices.
        6. A silver tea strainer was on another plate.
        7. On top of the folded cloth napkins were little spoons to stir the tea.

II Aunt Emily made delicious tea.
    A. First she prepared the pot.
        1. She heated water to warm the pot
        2. She heated water for tea as the other water was warming the teapot.
        3. She discarded the pot warming water and filled the pot with boiling water for tea

6 - Taming Wild Thoughts

  B. Next she added tea leaves to the water in the teapot.
    1. She put on the lid and let the leaves steep in the hot water
    2. She covered the teapot with a tea cosy to keep the pot warm.
    3. She placed the sliver tea strainer on the rim of the teacup and poured tea.
III Aunt Emily comes to visit
  A. She came to see her namesake.
  B. We had Cambric Tea
    1. This tea is blended with milk and sugar
    2. Jenifer Emily received her first sip of tea from a tiny spoon.
  C. Aunt Emily left a gift.
    1. She brought a dusty rose teapot for me to save for Jenifer Emily.
    2. She also left the little spoon from which Jenifer Emily and I had our first sips of tea.

* * *

TEA TIME - AUNT EMILY'S WAY

Sipping tea with Aunt Emily was a celebration of ceremony. Although she drank other beverages, a good cup of tea was by far her greatest pleasure. Whether Aunt Emily was in her own home or visiting family, she had sit down, enjoy a pot of tea twice a day.

She appeared each morning in a flowered dressing gown with her long hair flowing past her shoulders to the middle of her back. While she was waiting for water to boil, she carefully sectioned one half a grapefruit, then sprinkled it lavishly with sugar, placed it in a small grapefruit size, flowered china bowl. On weekdays, she toasted bread in the oven, but on Sunday she had an English muffin.

I was at her elbow watching everything. "Heidi dear," she'd say to me, "Please prepare the table."

"I have put out the placemats." I enjoyed this task because her placemats were hand embroidered and the delicate fabric was soft to the touch.

"Are the napkins in their rings?"

"I'll go see." Back to the dining room I would skip, pigtails bouncing. Before I could read, I learned to distinguish between the ornate silver napkin rings and put them at the appropriate places.

"Heidi, dear . . . the jelly, please." On toast days she had strawberry, blackberry, or sometimes special red raspberry preserves in a little pot with a tiny serving spoon. On Sunday, things were different. She topped her English muffin with orange marmalade served in a little glass pot with a silver top and silver spoon. Another job was to carry a plate with a fresh stick of butter to the table. On weekdays the butter was on a china plate, but for Sunday breakfast butter was on a glass plate. My final task was to place the New York Times, carefully folded in thirds, on the table to the left of the placemat.

As I was moving to and from the dining room, Emily was "setting the tea tray." For weekdays she used a simple silver tray. Usually the mat on the tea tray matched the place mats. Sunday, of course, was a more elaborate tray. There were the cups and saucers, the spoons, a saucer with lemon, a cream pitcher and a sugar bowl. The Sunday sugar was cubes. She had tiny pinchers that looked like bird claws to serve the cubes. The teapot, covered with a hand-embroidered cozy, sat to the right side of the tray. Beside the teapot was the tea strainer and bowl for tea leaves.

The time for afternoon was flexible, usually about four o'clock, after everyone awakened from napping. It was in the dining room and nearly as formal as breakfast tea, unless, of course, there were guests for tea, and then we moved to the living room. Those living room occasions sorely tested my teacup balancing skills and my ability to refrain from wiggling.

Afternoon tea was made and served from the tray in much the same way. The food was quite different in the afternoon. We had sugar cookies, nut cookies and sometimes dates stuffed with candied ginger. There were little finger sandwiches of egg salad and chicken or tuna salad on small soft circles and triangles of crustless white or whole wheat bread. Occasionally, instead of the sandwiches, there was Brie cheese with crackers.

On one occasion Aunt Emily knew my heart better than I as she suggested, "Heidi dear, if you feel as if you are about to suffer the wiggles, watch for the cheese under the glass dome to move. I am quite certain that it will relax and spread itself across the cheese board."

I watched the cheese, and it did relax! To cleanse our palates there was a dish of freshly sliced Comice pear or honeydew melon. Afternoon tea did not spoil appetites, because dinner was at eight o'clock.

Emily's tea was the best hot tea I have ever tasted. Her brewing method was simple. Heat the teapot with hot water. Discard the hot water. Measure by spoonfuls the loose tea. Pour hot water on the tea leaves, put on the top, cover the teapot and let it steep. She knew exactly when the tea was ready and served each cup, ceremoniously placing the strainer in the cup and pouring. She asked her guests how they would prefer their tea. Then, according to their wishes, she would add sugar and lemon or milk, stir and pass the tea to her guest directly from her tray. I had no choice. I was a child so I got "Cambric tea" served in a dainty blue and white cup and saucer with a demitasse spoon.

Aunt Emily came to visit me and to meet her baby great grandniece, my daughter, Jenifer Emily. The baby was about six months old. Of course we had tea. Over the years I suspected Cambric tea that I had grown to love while I was still very young, was actually warm milk and sugar with a little tea. I knew for sure about Cambric tea, as I watched Aunt Emily prepare it and spoon it to Jenifer Emily from the very demitasse spoon I had used when I visited her in New York City so long ago. She brought her dusty rose teapot wrapped in a towel for our tea. At the end of her visit Aunt Emily presented me with the special teapot and the tiny demitasse spoon for Jenifer Emily.

Notes

CHAPTER SEVEN:
Anecdote to Story

I was eleven when the first of my three brothers was born, and my life changed drastically. Because I was the extra mother and helped raise the boys until I went to college, I witnessed many of their antics. The oldest of the three, Andy, was the real handful. From early on we knew wherever people gathered, he sensed he had an audience, and it was show time. When my father and I took him to the grocery and pointed to a product, Andy sang the jingle and gave the commercial.

On one fateful trip to the grocery when he was two, Andy got his arm lodged in the cup dispenser chute of a drink machine. On another occasion he was separated from us in a department store during a shopping trip. We knew he was safe because the chuckling voice on the storewide loud speaker reported a lost little boy who said his name was Tennessee Ernie Ford. At night he went to bed Jimmy Durante style dressed in my grandfather's old hat, stopping in three imaginary spotlights to wave good night.

In the opening of this chapter the information I offer is anecdotal. The events are exactly those, events. The events would be a good basis for one or more stories. How do you get enough information from an event to create something with a beginning, middle and end? Stories need a setting, characters, and yes, action!

Storyteller and writer Sheila Kay Adams doesn't sit around smiling and nodding with folks and simply saying she remembers a day that butterflies landed on her face. That would be an anecdotal statement. In her book of stories, *Come Go Home With Me,* Adams skillfully weaves anecdotes into warmhearted stories by adding description, detail, dialogue, and plot. In her story "It's a Sign," she involves her readers in the details and events which lead up to the point when butterflies land on her face, and in her grandmother's reaction to that event. She builds gentle momentum as she builds her story. After chores, she and her Granny go into the woods to gather buckeyes. When that task is finished, they stop to ponder the minnows swimming in the creek. The momentum has been building in preparation for the high point of the story. Yellow butterflies arrive and land on her face. Her Granny is sure it is a sign. Adams tells her readers that over the years she returns to that spot hoping to see "a cloud of yellow." She also listens for the "rustle of a thousand little wings."

LifeLong Learner Eleanor Hill has collected anecdotal information about her childhood with her brothers. She could sit around with them and ask them if they remembered the time they put a crayfish in their grandfather's rain barrel. When they talk about the event, they probably sit around and make a few comments like how angry their grandfather was and how scared they were.

Remembering fragments is not the same as writing a story. Once the story is composed, the memory is alive forever. Hill has written an entertaining series of stories related to her brothers' tricks and practical jokes. After writing the stories, she joined a storytelling group and uses them as part of her storytelling repertoire.

Notice how she crafts her opening to draw you immediately into the story. She has a strong sense of place as she offers a setting rich in detail. Her characters are developed and enriched through carefully chosen detail. Notice, too, how she uses dialogue to move the story. Her dialogue also gives readers a peek at the children's personalities. There is rising action and finally the story comes to a climax when "Pap" comes face to face with the crayfish and Bob runs away. By introducing the parents at a strategic point, she is able to bring an interesting resolution to the plot and a satisfactory ending for the readers.

PAP'S RAIN BARREL

By

Eleanor Hill

We did put the crayfish in Pap's rain barrel and we knew he was going to kill all three of us. It all happened because we loved to play in the creek. The creek was a tranquil spring-fed stream running behind my grandparent's property and my two brothers and I loved to play in the cool water. We entertained ourselves for untold hours on steamy summer afternoons splashing and catching creatures. The water murmured as it rolled down stream and on hot summer afternoons it was a shady refuge. Crayfish resembling miniature lobsters lived under the rocks. Dragonflies with their iridescent wings swooped and dived above the water then hovered as though searching for a place to land.

It was a 10-hour trip to Pap's house and although the back seat of our '48 Buick Roadmaster was gigantic, it seemed to grow smaller with each mile. By the time we got to Pennsylvania we were bursting with energy and ecstatic to be free of the confinements of the car. We would explode from the car and head for the creek and freedom from adult supervision. One day we were having a glorious time horse playing in the water, turning over the cinnamon colored shale rocks, and chasing crayfish that dashed for cover, as their homes were uncovered.

Tom caught a huge crayfish, flipped it in my direction, and yelled, "Hey, Sis, catch this!"

I shrieked, "Tommy, don't! Quit it! Stop! I hate you."

"Hold on, I have an idea," he said in a hushed tone. "You know who is really scared of spiders and wiggly things?"

Bob and I answered whispering at precisely the same second, "Pap."

Tom said, "We could scare the bejeepers out of that fat old monster. Let's put crayfish in his rain barrel."

"No way," I pleaded. "We could get killed trying to scare him. He would know it was us."

"After all it is only a joke, and what's the

worst that could happen?" they chimed.

"The three of us getting caught and murdered on the spot," was my comeback. They persuaded me to go along with them and at least help catch the crayfish. I was more prudent when it came to releasing them into Pap's barrel and said. "No way. I will just watch."

Pap, our grandfather, was a grumpy despicable man, demanding and insensitive to my grandmother, and dictatorial with his grandchildren. He was enormous with a beer belly the size of a full term pregnancy. His voice was thunderous and he bellowed orders such as "Woman . . . beer" as he snapped his fingers over his head or "You kids better get out of here now." He drank beer continually and it was a relief when he finally drank enough to drift off, and began snoring like a steam engine. He appeared menacing with his heavy beard, double chins, and accusing gray eyes. To me he was the epitome of Billy Goat Gruff, and I was terrified of him.

He required my grandmother to bathe and shave him with rainwater. His barrel at the corner of the porch caught and held the sacred rainwater as it spilled from the downspout. He dared anyone to touch the water, the barrel, or the metal dipper hanging from its side. He demanded to be the first one seated at meals, and my grandmother was required to have his meat cut into bite size pieces before he sat down. Choice servings of everything on the table were his. When he wanted more food he would stab his fork at an empty place on his plate and grunt making the same noise an enormous hog makes at the trough rooting and snorting for the finest morsels.

We were thrilled to know the one imperfection in his cast iron armor. He was so afraid of spiders and creepy crawling things that when he needed to use the outhouse, my grandmother had to walk with him down the path. He stood outside while she went in with a rolled up newspaper and cleared all of the cobwebs and spider webs out of the corners and crevices. She stepped up on the seat to reach the ceiling and looked with her flashlight for any bugs, spiders or crawling creatures. Only then would Pap go in while she waited outside guarding against snakes that might crawl under the door.

The day the boys put the crayfish in the barrel, Pap came home from work as usual. After Granny had bathed him and put clean undershirt and socks on him, he came out to sit on the porch and wait for supper. We stood around for a while then began a game of tag, being careful to stay close enough to watch any action. Finally, Pap got up and walked over to his sacred barrel and picked up the dipper. He plunged it deep into the water for a cool drink. Just as he pulled the dipper up he looked down and let out a brutal roar. The dipper went airborne with water splashing all round, and a crayfish plopped on the porch floor. Pap staggered backwards and landed flat against the wall, the creature landed, scratching and wriggling its way across the linoleum. Earlier we were giggling and snickering, but now we were rooted in place watching this gigantic man cringe with fear and then transform himself into an irate animal. Fear contorted his face in alarm one second and then turned crimson from holding his breath. He began howling and the noise occupied all of space, it seemed to encompass the whole world.

As Granny came running out of the house, Pap was bellowing. "How did this happen?" Then came the horrible words, "I know who is responsible. . . . The three of you, get over here."

I tried to swallow, but my throat was constricted and my stomach felt like it was full of holes. Firing squad victims is what we were, standing there in a row waiting for the sound of the gun. Tears dropped onto my bare feet as we stood with our heads hung and eyes attached to our toes. I knew we were all going to die, Tom had finally gotten us into more trouble than even he could handle, and Mom and Dad were not here to stop what was about to take place.

Pap snarled, "OK, which one of you did this? You better own up to it now or all of you are going to get what is coming to you."

Tom squeaked. "I started it and Bob helped. I am sorry."

"Sorry," the old man stormed, "I will show

Keeper of the Stories

you sorry, you little weasel. You boys stand right where you are, and little girl, you get upstairs. Granny, get the strap."

I was halfway up the stairwell before Granny could get to the screen door handle. By the time she reached the hook where the razor strap was hung, I was standing at the top of the steps looking out the window. I heard the door slam as she went out and saw Tom and Bob running down the path to the creek. They hit the water on a dead run, turned left up the creek, and disappeared under the overhanging trees.

Pap was charging after them swinging the strap and yelling, "Get back here you sneaky little brats. So help me God, you are going to get what you deserve this time."

It seemed like an eternity before I heard the car door slam. Mom and Dad arrived. Pap met them halfway to the house bellowing, "You will not believe what those damn boys of yours have done this time."

Dad shouted, "Calm down, Pap, and tell me what in the name of Hell has happened."

Pap was in such a rage he was incoherent so Granny related the whole hideous story. Dad went down to the creek and called but there was to answer from the boys. Later we sat down to eat, but I could not swallow, so I was staring out the window, saw Bob down at the creek shifting from one foot to the other as he glanced towards the house. Dad finished eating then he strolled out to where Bob was still twisting in anguish. I can only guess the interaction from their body language.

It was obvious Dad was saying, "Bob you have really screwed up with the old man. What in the name of God possessed you two to bait that old goat? You know he is terrified beyond belief of crawling things, and you know he has a boiling temper. I will give it to you; I would never have been brave enough to cross him."

Bob's head was bobbing up and down and he looked like those little plastic animals sitting in the rear window of cars with their heads wobbling around. He was agreeing with every word of Dad's discourse and as they came within earshot, I heard Bob say, "Is it safe to go in the house? I will apologize and promise to never do anything like that again and I will take whatever punishment you think is fair but please don't let him beat me with the strap."

Dad said, "You go on in and go to bed. The old man has had his quota of beer and he is in there rattling the walls with his snoring. Just stay out of his sight until tomorrow when things have calmed down."

Pap left for work the next morning and Tom still had not come back to the house. He had spent the night in a cow barn upstream and Dad found him walking out of the pasture. He convinced Tom that he would not be tortured or killed and brought

Keeper of the Stories

him back to the house.

Dad and Pap worked out some work details for the boys. They were so relieved to not receive any bodily injury they were willing to answer "Yes Sir" to any demands Pap made for the rest of our visit. They did not balk at shoveling out the hen house, hoeing and weeding the garden, cutting the grass on the whole three acres or painting the outhouse.

I know I thanked My Heavenly Father that I did not participate in dropping those critters into that barrel. I also remember what a blissful feeling it was when the crayfish episode was over and we were able to return to our tranquil little creek to roughhouse and splash around in the cool water

What began as reminiscences for Hill turned into a solid story with characters, setting, dialogue and plot. On the surface the story seems to be pranks of childhood, there is a subtle message about family dynamics and interaction between the generations. Give yourself permission, as Hill did, to recall difficult family situations with humor. In time darker memories are erased with laughter and life is easier. You can write a good solid story. Now is the time to begin!

CHAPTER EIGHT:
Narrative Nightmares

As if organizing your story material were not enough, you must make an important decision as you prepare to write. Who will tell the story? Will you present the story from your point of view? Will you choose a person who is central to the story or someone else who is not directly involved, to tell the story? No matter from which point of view your family story is told, your story is bound to be successful and filled with personal insight, if you remember the sage, often quoted words of Atticus Finch to his daughter, Scout, in Harper Lee's novel, *To Kill A Mockingbird.* "You never really understand a person until you consider things from his point of view . . . until you climb into his skin and walk around in it."

Understanding a few germane terms is a prelude to point of view selection. The words "narrative", "narration", and "narrator," which are related by a common root, sound similar; yet, without definition they may be confusing.

Narrative - This term may relate to fiction, nonfiction, poetry, or drama. It is an account or story of an event or a series of events. A good example of personal narrative would be the fictitious yet historic work, *Journal of the Plague Year* by Daniel Defoe, an 18th Century British writer. Defoe, originally a journalist, enjoyed history so much that he created his own version of an historical event. He fabricated a first person account of someone who supposedly experienced the Great Plague of 1665, which ravaged London, and lived to tell about it. Even with archaic language in places, Defoe's *Journal of the Plague Year* is engrossing reading and offers a peek into life in England during 1665.

Narration - This is the act of telling the story. Often people think of telling a story in terms of the spoken word. That is storytelling in the oral tradition. Narration can take the written form, too. The written narration form is used in autobiographies, biographies, and memoir. Narration works for stories as well as book-length works; therefore, the length does not matter. Often the popular format for writing life stories is chronological sequence to structure the work.

Flashbacks and foreshadowing are interesting techniques that may be used to impart information as the story progresses.

Remembrance might be a more comfortable term than flashback. The remembrance is something that happens prior to the beginning of this particular story, and can gracefully interrupt the ongoing story to give some information. Dreams or daydreams of the person telling the story are simple ways to work in a remembrance. The verb tense for a remembrance should be past tense. Transitional phrases such as "He remembered the time when . . . " or, "She was familiar with the sound. It was just like . . . " or, "The laughter I heard was so much like my mother's the time we . . . " Using italics is a visual way to remind readers that this is a remembrance, not what is happening now.

Foreshadowing sounds like a mysterious term. Foreshadowing does not dip into the past, but it is a signal, a clue of things to come. An example of foreshadowing might go somewhat like this:

> As many times as Mother and I climbed the steps up from the beach to the house, I never saw her need to stop and catch her breath. Today, she stopped.

By indicating something out of the ordinary, you signal to your readers that something is about to change.

An interesting literary gem tucked between remembrance and foreshadowing is *interior monologue.* Through interior monologue you let your readers eavesdrop in the mind of the person. This takes place in the present and is easiest to do from first person point of view. As the story progresses on the outside, the character is thinking something quite different, and is having an internal conversation with himself or herself. This technique is fairly easy to write, and can help move the story along as well as let your readers know more about the character. Have you ever attended a gathering, and while you are chatting with a guest, your mind wanders? Perhaps you are thinking you should have worn more comfortable shoes, put on a tie instead of a sweater, or wondered about a very familiar, much older lady on the arm of a yet-to-be identified young man, and at the same time you politely converse with another guest? There you have interior monologue!

Narrator - This is the teller of the story. It could be the author, or it could be one of the characters in the story. In developing and writing life stories or family stories, try not to automatically assume the yoke of responsibility that you, the author, must be the teller.

Do you want to tell the story from an "I" perspective? The choice is yours. The "I" can be you, or it can be your character. Then you will be using a *"first person"* narrator. Using an *unreliable narrator* to tell the story, having freedom to choose the voice and personal perspective of a specific narrator, and having easy access to the character's thoughts are three advantages to writing your story using first person point of view.

You can establish a rapport with your readers because they always know who is seeing and interpreting the narrative action. Suppose you choose to write about yearly pilgrimage you and your family made to the beach. Using first person, you might say something like this:

> My sister and I got up every morning just as the ruby sun peeked above the horizon. Carrying my shell bag and a banana, I constantly waited for slowpoke Angela. We tiptoed out of the beach house, through the dune grasses to the beach to hunt for shells. I loved the cool damp sand on soles of my feet.

Because the point of view is first person, readers know what "I" thinks, but cannot know Angela's thoughts.

There is always a chance that the first person narrator proves to be offering unreliable information. Your narrator could be a hypocrite. An example could be the way Uncle Harry talks about house hunting. He tried to get a bank loan to buy his dream house, but his loan application was rejected. As he tells the story, he leads people to believe he really doesn't care that he didn't get the loan. He claims it doesn't matter at all. He doesn't like steps, and the house was a two-story structure, and he really didn't want it anyway.

The first-person narrator can also prove unreliable by giving misleading information. Suppose Auntie Clara, the queen of malapropos, says she attended the annual Fourth of July festivities at the county fairgrounds. You are comfortable believing her.

> After the picnic lunch and jump rope games with the other girls, I looked forward to the parade. When the band played, I marched in place as I watched the soldiers in full dress uniform manuring all over the field

Although you have written of that incident, your readers know that it is Auntie Clara's account of the event. It is not your word choice mistake or a spelling error. Your readers accept the peculiar error, because the source of the error is Auntie Clara, the narrator, not the author.

Another advantage to first person point of view is the freedom you have to choose a voice. Although you may be well educated, the person telling the story may not speak with perfect grammar or may show an affinity to slang. The variations are acceptable because these are not shortcomings of you, the writer, but those of your character's voice. Getting into dialect, grammatical errors and slang is rather tricky. There is always the question of how much is enough. If you are trying to capture the essence of the person's speech, sprinkle the variations gently and with great care. Nothing is worse than to be reading an interesting life story only to be overwhelmed to the point of distraction by having to stumble over and figure out dialect or grammar errors. So while remaining true to your character, remember, in this case less is better!

A final advantage to first person point of view

Keeper of the Stories

is your readers' direct and easy access to the character's thoughts.

To get the full picture before making a point of view decision, you must know that there are a few disadvantages to using first person point of view.

It is difficult to get any type of physical description or exterior view of your character. And writing straightforward dialogue is challenging. If "I" tells the story, you the writer sometimes have a difficult time creating a little bit of dramatic momentum or suspense when "I" gets in a tough spot, because it is obvious since "I" tells the story, "I" made it through the situation.

Another interesting option is to write the story from an *omniscient* point of view. You are the "all knowing" author. There are some advantages to being all-knowing. Depending, of course, on the amount of information you have about the people as you shape the family story, you can use their names, get into the thoughts of all the characters and at the same time remain objective. As you write, when you don't use the proper names, you use the third person pronouns such as he, she, it, and they.

In writing family stories, point of view can be enlightening to you and other family members. No one has the same view of what happened. Unless you are seeking the absolute truth about something, don't be concerned if family members squawk a bit that, in their opinion, you just didn't get it right.

Writing Assignment

Here is the situation: It is late in the afternoon, and you have to make a quick trip to the market. Juggling packages, groping for keys as you approach your car, you see a teen driver back her car into your car and lock bumpers. The girl calls the police from her cell phone, and you both wait for the police.

1. Write a fictional account of the accident from your point of view, including an accident-related flashback, as you wait for the policeman. With a yellow highlight pen underline the statements which represent your viewpoint. This will help you see if you have shifted to another point of view or have created a confusing point of view.

2. Rewrite the account of the accident by adding a hint of foreshadowing. Here is a sample foreshadowing sentence: "Things had not been going right all day." As you are being polite to the flustered young woman, reveal what is also going on inside your head.

3. Rewrite the accident from an omniscient/all knowing point of view. You are the camera reporting only what you see. Remember there is no way for you know what is going on inside the woman and the girl. Report only on what appears to be. You will need yellow and green highlighting pens. Highlight all that represents your point of view in yellow and highlight all that represents the girl's point of view in green. Are both points of view clear?

4. Suggest a "group write" at a time when family members are gathered. Select a topic that will be a specific, possibly controversial family event. A story that begs to be written by various members of my family concerns the great "Don't Drop Your Ice Cream Caper." Although it happened over twenty years ago, they discuss it as if it had happened last summer. It is almost a story just to set up the differing opinions of the event as a writing sample:

Each summer, since the youngest child was one year old, we have spent our summers on the Outer Banks of North Carolina. It seems that on the hottest nights our four children loved nothing better than to cavort on the sand dunes of Jockey's Ridge and then load up in their dad's pickup truck to go for ice cream cones. One night just as Jenny received her double-dip chocolate chip ice cream piled high on a sugar cone, the server said to the little girl with the big cone, "Don't drop your ice cream." With that, the ice cream toppled from the cone onto the gravel parking lot.

That moment was forever frozen into our family history. From there the story takes on many variations:

Jenny claims one of her three sandy brothers crowded her, bumped her elbow, therefore causing the ice cream to fall.

The brother who had already been served was convinced his sister turned too fast because she was trying to beat him back to the truck to get the highly prized seat in the spare tire, the seat he was ready to take.

I saw her take a lick to stop the melting ice cream from running down the cone onto her sandy hand and up her forearm. She licked from the bottom of the ice cream towards the top, the ice cream wobbled, and down it went.

Then the youngest shouted for all the ice cream eaters in the parking lot to hear, "She dropped her ice cream." The server took pity, and Jenny got a free ice cream cone. She chose a different flavor.

The disgruntled brother, unhappy with his flavor selection, complained that she dropped her ice cream on purpose because she wanted another flavor. But that is another story!

Do you see how a shared event can take on many variations? Pass the lemonade, and share the stories!

Notes

CHAPTER NINE:
Great Beginnings and Endings

In every sense of the word, it is now "show time." Your ideas are ready to become a work in progress.

In the Beginning . . .

How do you grab your readers, keep them interested beyond the first page? It is simple. Begin with an image that will create an immediate urge to read on.

But how do you do that?

Example: If you choose to write about the time that your family got its first television set, possibly the first television set in the neighborhood, you could begin this way:

> A few decades ago when I was about 10 years old, we got our first television set.

Or, you could give your readers the one-two punch

with something like this:

> Things really changed in my home the summer I had my tenth birthday. The Korean War was over, my brother went to college on the GI bill, and my dad bought a television set.

Although the improved beginning may need polishing, it will generate much more reader interest than

"A few decades ago . . . "   {{{{ *yawn* }}}}

As you read the revised beginning do you recall things about the Korean War? Was your family affected in any way by the war? Do you recall your first television set? Was it one of those ten-inch black and white flickering miracles? Did your dad block the view for at least half the program as he adjusted the contrast or brightness of the picture? Was someone always rearranging the "rabbit ears" to get rid of the two or three shadows on the people or snow-like appearance of the picture? Do you remember Morton Downey at the organ and Kate Smith's fifteen-minute music program? Did Captain Video, Kukla, Fran and Ollie, or Howdy Doody entertain you? Then there was *The Ed Sullivan Show*, which brought Elvis Presley and The Beatles as well as other music, dance, and comedy to Sunday evening television viewers. The supporting details for the beginning of your story are limitless as you let your mind drift to the earlier time.

In the following pages, I offer several suggestions for good beginnings and endings. The bottom line is that the final decision as how to begin your work is up to you. Write your piece with a beginning you like at the time, but know that after the first draft

9 - Great Beginnings and Endings

of your work is finished, you may choose to alter or even delete the beginning. You might find that the best opening lines are two or three paragraphs into the work. Don't hesitate to experiment.

I have prepared in no particular order of preference a list of suggestions for ways to begin your work.

* Setting

Opening with setting is frequently used, but can be an effective and interesting beginning. An advantage to opening with setting is that after reading your description, your readers will be ready to share the same sense of place. You have prepared your readers to meet the people and experience the events in your story. You have flexibility and freedom within the setting convention.

Rather than a general description of a room, a house, or a geographical place, add a variation. Consider offering your description from the vantage point of just arriving at the place. Have you left the interstate and taken the small state route into the town? How have things changed? Are you going back to the old and abandoned farmhouse belonging to your grandparents? Take your readers down the gravel lane, up the rotting wooden steps, push open the knobless wooden front door and let the adventure unfold. Lure your readers into wanting to know more details.

Your setting could be a departure from a location instead of an arrival. Consider sequences such as packing the car, consulting the map, looking out the rear view mirror at the house, town, or landscape. Will you or another person be saddened by the departure? Once again, tease your readers into wanting to turn the page, wanting to know more about why you have chosen to depart this carefully described place.

Not only did Bob Kelly begin "Thunder in the Basement" (see Chapter Five) with a setting, but he also included amazing facts about Tacoma, Washington:

> I grew up in Tacoma, Washington. Tacoma was the lumber capital of the world in the early 1900s having more sawmills and producing more finished lumber than any other place in the universe. Forests of Douglas fir that surrounded the city stretched into the Cascade Mountains. Sawmills lined Tacoma's waterfront, and ships moored at their piers to load and carry lumber to the ends of the earth. Lumber was king and that influenced my life in many ways.

* *Strong Sensory Image*

For a sensual opening, now is the time to consider the five senses. Smelling, tasting, seeing, hearing, or touching will tantalize, draw your readers into the work. This type of opening brings the sensual side of your readers to the story. Whenever I smell grilled onions and green peppers, I am flooded with memories. I recall my visits to county fairs at the end of summer. I have many green pepper and onion memories surrounding my days as a student teacher in Marietta, Ohio. On bitterly cold winter days after a day of teaching at the local high school. I passed a tiny mom-and-pop-style restaurant as I trudged back to the campus of Marietta College. Nearly every day the aroma of peppers and onions on the grill beckoned me to step inside for a bite to eat.

Suppose you had an extraordinarily rainy summer vacation and you wish to tell the tale, maybe embellish a little. Perhaps you choose to write a creative nonfiction piece about life before air conditioning.

> It is the time before air conditioning, you are visiting a relative and you are sweltering in a dark bedroom, perspiring so that you taste the saltiness on your upper lip. You wrestle with the clinging sheets, thump the musty pillow, the oscillating fan creaks at each left sweep, and then in the darkness, you hear a whining mosquito.

The sensory opportunities are boundless.
Sometimes less is more when writing description. Remember, carefully selected verbs are more effective than a heaping helping of adverbs and adjectives. See the discussion of word choice in the Appendix.

*Need or Motive
This is a prime opportunity to introduce a person—the subject of your writing. Perhaps an event has occurred to make the person want something. What does the person lack that he or she desires, demands, or requires? You have an opportunity to grab your readers' attention by surprise or shock. It can be in the form of a simple statement. If you can use humor to establish the need or motive so much the better. A desire for a good meal, searching for a reliable automobile, or a surprising change in attitude can present an intriguing or humorous opening:

> As my three brothers were going through the long hair stage of the seventies, our conventional mother needed a rationale for accepting the fact that in spite of the long hair, my brothers' attitudes were good, their grades were not dropping, and the end of the world was not imminent. That led to her epiphany about hair. She issued her classic state-

ment of the seventies: "Hairstyle is a personal preference and does not indicate lack of character."

Although the following statement is not humorous, it is full of intrigue and possibilities and certainly would grab your readers' attention:

> All I want is to live in one place and stay in one school long enough, so I can take driver education and get my license."

This is not necessarily a shocking statement. The true and compelling words were said a decade ago by a young man who sat in the front row in my tenth-grade English class for a few weeks. I am not certain that he ever achieved his goal, for about three years after he was taken from my class, placed in other foster homes, and enrolled in other schools, he was found murdered under a bridge.

I have often wondered if I could ever do enough research to answer some of the questions presented by his statement. Perhaps I could use his statement as a starting point and take a general look at other children in foster home situations, some which proved to be successful, some which did not work. I would take the topic from general to specific.

Ann Falcone Shalaski bombards the senses with images, sights, and sounds of a diner long past its prime. The following is the opening of "The Tennessee Waltz" (Her complete text can be found in Chapter Eleven).

> The diner was empty. Easing into a booth, wiping mottled dust from the table, I felt uneasy as the storm continued to hammer the metal roof like

kettledrum, and wind slapped waves of rain flooding the grimy windows. Condensation spilled over the sills and down the faded blue walls. Floral plastic curtains, brittle and cracked, did little to improve the bleak surroundings. It was Sunday, a day for families, togetherness and love, not my favorite day.

* *Prediction*

You can tease your readers with the prediction then hook them into reading more to see if the prediction comes true. Shakespeare was no stranger to employing predictions and prophecies. The witches in Shakespeare's play *Macbeth* prophesy that Banquo, Macbeth's friend, will be the father of future kings: "Thou shalt get kings though thou be none." In *Julius Caesar*, the old soothsayer warns Caesar, "Beware the ides of March." Nostradamus, a 16th Century physician and astrologer, wrote a volume of prophecies in verse. To this day curious writers and others dip into his prophecies as they try to interpret what may become of the world. The luster of prophecy endures.

Books and articles were written about the predictions of dire things that would happen when the world went from 1999 to 2000. Probably every family has memories of the moving into the new millennium. There were no massive blackouts, no planes dropped from the sky, and bottled water disappeared from grocery shelves as many families celebrated the new millennium. Did your family prepare?

Perhaps a family member has a surefire way of predicting the sex of an unborn child. Is there a relative in your family who has prophetic dreams? There may be a relative who could sense impending doom and did so on a regular basis. When I was little, my grandmother would predict a critical injury each time I climbed the old willow tree. "You are going to fall out of that tree one day and break your neck." An essay could branch in many directions from her warning. It could profile her cautions nature, encompass many controlling, yet charming colloquialisms, or serve as a prediction of my yet to come, somewhat freewheeling youth. Maybe there is a family time capsule with predictions from long ago about to be opened. An interesting opening could focus on one of the predictions.

* Symbolic Object

Symbols are everywhere. Search your mind and closet with a creative eye. When you choose to open with a symbolic object, select one that illustrates the idea you wish to convey. Think of hawks and doves as birds. Review their attributes. Can those attributes be applied to people? In times of war there are many congressional debates between the "hawks" and "doves." Do you have a relative with a "hawkish-warlike" personality always ready for a good argument to help you see the picture the right way? In your family is there a "dove-like" relative who loves peace, strives for world peace as well as personal peace?

For example:

> I know an older woman who inherited her Victorian grandmother's mourning bonnet. Evidently, the grandmother became a widow while she was still quite young. For decades she passed through the various stages of mourning according to the expected social custom in Victorian times. The bonnet, symbolic of grieving, could lead to a general

essay on mourning etiquette and the proper clothing dictated by the stage of mourning, as inspired by Queen Victoria, who languished over the loss of her beloved Albert. Still using the symbolic mourning bonnet as the subject, the essay could reflect the lifestyle of a Victorian woman widowed at an early age. It could be very personally related to one special grandmother.

Another example:

My father believed that as long as people maintained a sense of humor and retained the ability to smile, all would be well. There were times when my feverish, upchucking little brothers were flat out in bed. Daddy would come home from work and relentlessly entertain until he got a smile from the sickest child. "There, you see," he would say, "he smiled, he's getting better." The smile for Daddy was symbolic of returning to normal. Years later, a heart attack took him quite suddenly. Daddy, my brothers and I had been out to dinner in his favorite German restaurant the week before he died. I went home for the funeral, and we all went out to dinner to celebrate Daddy's spirit. Once more we dined at his favorite German restaurant. The waitress seated us and said, "Will your father be joining your party?" It was a strange moment. Then we looked at each other and began to laugh. "Well, not exactly," we told the waitress. "He died Tuesday." She was flabbergasted, but we continued to smile. "Don't worry, he's with us," we said. We were smiling; the healing had begun.

* *Person Portrait*

Here is your opportunity to open your work by word painting the features and qualities of a person. Reformulate the old adage that a picture is worth a thousand words to be more creative. Description paints a good picture. This successful beginning, a personal description of your subject, might turn tedious unless your descriptions are fresh. If there is one blue eye and one green, you might have something. Comparing the person's voice to a foghorn is overused. You may imply the same idea but in fresh terms: "His voice is so husky it could guide a ship to port in a storm." Is the person wealthy? You could say she was as rich as Fort Knox, but you would be using a tired comparison. Find another way to convey wealth: "By the time I met Aunt Anna, she was so wealthy she could buy the bank."

Fashion trends can be translated into images. Making reference to a classic brand name will bring understanding to the word portrait. Who is to say how a trend gets started? Sometimes it is with a musical group. Remember the Beatles and the popularity of the Liverpool bowl-cut hair? Decades later, a musical movement in Seattle, WA yielded a clothing trend that sent manufacturers scurrying to keep up with demand for oversize, baggy clothing. It was called the Grunge look. To say that he is classic "Seattle Grunge" will imply the image of drab colors, big shirts, and loose pants cut off at mid-calf. For three decades many folks enjoyed music and shows put on by a group of musicians called The Grateful Dead.

9 - Great Beginnings and Endings

The band followers were called "Deadheads." Think "Deadhead" and envision love beads, head scarves, and colorful tie-dyed garments.

Sometimes brand names denote a style: "He was a Brooks Brothers man," or, "She was a pearls and Pendleton Plaid girl" speaks to the other end of the fashion and interest spectrum. After you consult the discussion of redundancy and the list of cringing clichés in the Appendix, you will move towards fresh, solid ground with your descriptions.

In the End . . .

Just as a good beginning can get you going, a good ending can bring satisfying closure to your story. Do not rush to complete the story. Be consistent by writing at the same pace and in the same style as you did in the beginning and the middle of the work. It might be that you want to leave your readers desiring to read more, but please don't leave them unsatisfied with a weak or abrupt ending. Even if the ending is not roses and laughter, write it. I know very few folks who enjoy reading a story that has no definitive end.

So, as you approach the end of your piece, consider the final impression you wish to leave with your readers. Here are two simple ways to end your story that should be easy for you to implement and at the same time please your readers.

* *Circular ending*

With a circular ending, you conclude your story with the same idea or topic as you used for the beginning of the piece. There is reader satisfaction in being brought up to date. If you start with a symbol such as the mourning bonnet, you could come full circle and reveal the current status of the bonnet. You could include such information as the preservation method, and where it is stored. Folks are curious about antique items. There is a sentimental value, but is there also an appraised value? The current owner may have a plan for the bonnet's future. It could be willed to a relative, put on permanent loan at a museum, or sold to an antique dealer.

A circular ending also works well if you have opened your story with a setting, a description of a person, a prophecy or a tradition. Your readers are interested to see if time and events have changed the setting, whether and how the character has been affected, if or when the prophecy was fulfilled, or if a tradition has continued through the generations.

In Chapter Five, Elsie Duval comes full circle with "Corsages." Her beginning was a 1930s corsage observation and ended with her 1990s observation. Here is the final paragraph:

> I glanced around St. Andrew's Episcopal Church last Easter Sunday just to see how many women were wearing corsages in the 1990s. After a quick head count, I concluded that today's florists must make their living by selling potted plants. In spite of it all, there was one precious 90-year-old widow sprinting down the aisle with a white orchid pinned to her purse. I felt sure this was one girl who never ever once in her lifetime would have stomped a corsage to death.

* Sensory Image

This is one way to leave a lasting impression. As you bring your story to an end with images that appeal to the senses, you leave your readers with a concrete idea. For the ending of "Pap's Rain Barrel" found in Chapter

9 - Great Beginnings and Endings

Seven, Eleanor Hill uses sensory image. She concludes with an image of children at play after the crisis is over. Here is the last paragraph from "Pap's Rain Barrel:"

> I know I thanked My Heavenly Father that I did not participate in dropping those critters into that barrel. I also remember what a blissful feeling it was when the crayfish episode was over and we were able to return to our tranquil little creek to roughhouse and splash around in the cool water.

* *Epilogue*

Occasionally, you may have completed the story but feel that there is still a little bit more to say or an explanation is needed about something in the story. This is the time for a epilogue. John Sampson included an epilogue to his story, "Shamrocks and Roses" (The complete text can be found in Chapter Eleven):

> "Rhoda, I have just finished my garage is a mess story. Will you read it?" I ask as Rhoda passes my study door. "Any comments will be appreciated."
>
> "I suppose it is about my red roses."
>
> "Well, yes it is." She takes the story and disappears down the hall.
>
> Rhoda reappears, her face is flushed. "This isn't right! You talk about my things in the garage, and there's nothing about your things, like all those shelves of hazardous products you have out there."
>
> "What hazardous products?"
>
> "All those gallons of old house paint. If you threw them out you could get most of the things up

off the floor and on those shelves including the boxes. And what's more, my roses have been in the garage just four days while your mess has been there for forty years."

I blanch. Rhoda is right. Eighty percent of the stuff in the garage is mine. And I hereby resolve to clean it up the day school is out, unless I am too busy in the yard or writing stories like this.

Other possibilities for endings should be mentioned.

"Open-ended" endings leave the door open to more for stories with a similar theme.

Summaries recapitulate what has happened in the story. You might find that bringing an ending to a family story using a summary ending is tedious writing and equally tedious reading.

Trick endings and *surprise endings* work better in fiction writing; also, if the ending of the story is not well written, your readers might be confused and actually miss the point you worked so hard to make.

In your box of writer tools you have several options to end your story. A word of caution is needed to encourage you to avoid temptation:

You must vow never, *ever* to use the following classic sentence to end you story:

"They lived happily ever after."

CHAPTER TEN:
Speak To Me

Fiction writers are not the only writers who struggle with dialogue. Dialogue has a place in creative nonfiction writing as well. Whether you are writing stories about folks living or dead, you will want them to speak. You may not be able to attribute a direct quote to a person long gone; however, take heart, for you can allow the person to participate in conversations. Although it isn't authentic speech, dialogue sounds as if it were a real conversation. Well-written dialogue can make a particular point and contribute greatly to your story. Don't be tempted to use dialogue as a way to fill space.

Think of narrative and dialogue as a team. Narrative describes the people or characters, but dialogue gives them substance. Dialogue humanizes and firmly establishes identity. To give your people credibility, you put words that they would say in their mouths. If your uncle is well educated, it would be out of character for him to be continually grammatically incorrect—or, even worse, speak in clichés and slang.

Because I was very young, I can't remember the exact words my soft-spoken grandfather used when discussing his dislike for Franklin D. Roosevelt's administration. I do recall his dislike for the man. My grandfather, a superintendent at an Ohio glass plant, a patriotic American, and a staunch Republican, had political opinions which are legendary in our family. Without knowing word for word what he said, I could set up a typical dinner table dialogue he might have with my grandmother. He and my grandmother might have conversed in this manner during a typical dinner discussion. Then, being true to my grandfather's opinions I would create the following dialogue:

"Heidi, please call your grandfather to supper," my grandmother said. As she spoke, we heard a scuffling, grumbling, and paper crumpling in the living room. We looked at each other. She sighed and untied her apron. "It appears your grandfather has chosen to read the newspaper before supper tonight."

"Should I still call him?"

"Well dear, he has already crumbled the paper. Go ahead, but don't mention the newspaper."

During supper, my mother, her two sisters, my grandparents, and I sat in silence around the oval dining table. Knives and forks clinked on the plates. As we chewed, we looked at each other and smiled. Sometimes Aunt Janey winked at me as we waited for words we knew would surely come. My grandfather carefully placed his knife and fork side-by-side on his plate as he looked at my grandmother. "That man is sending our economy to Hell in a hand basket!"

After his pronouncement, the remainder of our dinner was pleasant, and nobody discussed "that man." I learned very quickly not to ask the identity of "that man," for the man was FDR.

Remember as you write dialogue, each person in your story deserves a strong voice. Some people speak in complete sentences while others tend to talk in sentence fragments. How do your people speak? The diction can be revealing. Through word choice you can inform your readers about the social class, region of the country, education, way of thinking for each one of your people. Here is a note of caution:

It is important to watch not only *what* your people say, but *how* they say it.

Dialect is a vehicle for enhancing the personality. If you wish to portray a certain dialect or speech pattern in your person's conversation, refrain from unusual spelling. As you will see in the following example, silly spelling is a distraction.

"Air ye deef?" the old woman muttered.

If it be known, the old man was just plain bereft of gumption. "I jest hain't been a wantin' to be a heerin' ye."

A more readable version would be:

"Are ye deaf?" the old woman muttered.

If the truth must be known, the old man was lacking gumption. "I ain't been wanting to hear ye."

Every word need not be in dialect. First, stick with dialect that is familiar to you. Then, remain consistent throughout your work by using one or two well-crafted examples as needed. Consistently using "ye" for "you" will remind your readers that the folks are not cosmopolitan. While "ain't" is not recognized as standard English, it can be used within reason if you are writing of someone with "ain't" as a part of the vocabulary.

Don't let dialogue intimidate you. At first, you may feel like a juggler as you realize when writing dialogue, you could be accomplishing many things at the same time. Through dialogue you will be able to:

* Develop your people
* Set the scene
* Advance the plot
* Foreshadow an event

The following tips about the forms that dialogue can take should dispel the mystery of writing effective dialogue:

* *Conversation*

Because dialogue is conversation, the characters talk to each other, so they should sound like real people. It would seem that all you have to do is listen to people and write their conversations word for word. That just doesn't work. You can transcribe their words, possibly through description capture basic body language, but you can't get the subtle nuances of tone and inflection of the speaker's voice. In print it is impossible to convey two people speaking at the same time.

This might be a typical conversation:

"Where do you live?"
"711 Windy Drive"

Now, notice how bland conversation becomes a bit more interesting when it becomes dialogue:

> "Where do you live?"
> "Over there on Windy Drive. I just moved into that old, gray house, if you want to call that a house."

* Provide Information

Imagine that your story is a period piece set during the Revolutionary War. You might want some historical background, commentary about the geography of the land, philosophy of the time, a sample of honor or loyalty. These things are best introduced in a narrative summary rather than through dialogue. Your story will drag, and the conversation will probably seem stilted and artificial. Since it is people talking, not journalists reporting the news, your people should come to life through their dialogue. It is easy to become wordy and slip unnecessary information into the dialogue, so summarize nonessentials in narrative, then get on with the action through your dialogue:

> The general did not seem concerned that the scouting reports indicated a large salt marsh area his soldiers had to ford during the march from Williamsburg to Yorktown. A large military battle was coming, but nobody, not even the general, knew the natural dangers that lay ahead as the soldiers set out. It was mid-October and unusually warm. The salt marsh mosquitoes began their feast. Mosquitoes attacked faces, necks, hands and every area of the soldiers' exposed flesh. The young drummer's hands were black with the swarming insects.

Keeper of the Stories

"Increase the cadence," the general commanded. There was silence. Not a drumbeat to be heard. "Increase the cadence. That's an order!" The general bellowed his instructions, and in an unusual move, he rode to see why the drummer was silent and out of step.

"Sir," the drummer said, holding his hands for the general to inspect. His fingers were swollen fat as sausages. "My hands are swelled, and I cannot hold the drumsticks."

* *Establish a setting*

This is an interesting and effective way to reveal the setting, the mood, the tone, and the atmosphere for your story. Suppose you want to establish an unpleasant tone. YOU put ominous words in the mouth of your characters and place the people in a foreboding location. Try this bit of dialogue:

"Dad, I'm so scared. My teeth are chattering, and my knees are wobbly."

I heard my father's raspy whisper. "Stay still. The rattlesnake is still in striking range."

"I can't stay still one more minute."

"Do as I say!"

* *Show a physical/psychological characteristic*

You might have one person out of harmony (a direct contrast) with the background. A humorous yet poignant essay rich in dialogue could come from the lives of the workers in my father's warehouse. During the Hungarian Revolution, many refugees came to my town in West Virginia. My father was president of a wholesale hardware distributing company, and Daddy hired a college professor to work in the warehouse while the man learned English. He also hired a woman, a concert pianist with five young sons. She had fled Hungary leaving everything behind, but maintained faith for new beginning in America. She worked while she learned English, and stayed with for my father as office manager until the business closed. Her five sons graduated from college. Many had multiple postgraduate degrees.

An interesting story would be about the way the warehouse workers, somewhat fearful of the non-English speaking strangers, spoke very loudly to the refugees as though sheer volume would serve as translator, how they came to terms with their differences, and eventually shared all they had with the refugees.

Psychological setting can be established and enriched by showing character conflict through dialogue. Spend time contemplating and understanding the internal makeup of your person. When you understand your subject, you can portray anger, motivation, pain, and other emotions through dialogue. You will be able to reveal the values, motivation, and methods of coping used by your people. If you are writing of an ancestor, you might read old letters and journals. If no personal documents are available, read period newspapers, other publications, and public documents to get a feel for issues and public opinions. With pieces of research, you could create believable dialogue.

* *Move the plot*

Although your family story may be brief, it has a beginning, middle and end. The plot, nestled in the middle of your story, is the backbone of your story. If this were a textbook, plot would warrant a chapter. In fact, there are books entirely devoted to plot. If you are motivated to study rising action, climax or moment of enlightenment, and resolution, which are all elements of the plot, the information is available. Narrative and dialogue can work hand in hand. Although narrative description of emotions such as ambition, fear, love, anger, jealousy, etc., can advance the plot, dialogue will move the plot, too. Sometimes a portion of narrative may indicate foreshadowing, a brief dialogue exchange may accomplish the same sense of foreshadowing in far less words or time. Carefully crafted dialogue may actually inject life into a weak plot. The foreshadowing technique bolsters a wobbly plot as it hints of good or unpleasant events to come. This is not a difficult technique. The following dialogue waves the red flag to readers, saying that more struggles are to come for Aunt Mable and Uncle George.

> It was late August, and Aunt Mable dabbed at the perspiration on her upper lip with the last of her lacy linen handkerchiefs. "The garden is so dry. Nothing but a few tomatoes to put up this summer. What are we going to do in winter?"
>
> "Mable, first things first," Uncle George said. "I need to get the car running."
>
> "Oh George, I have begun to feel that a big black cloud is hanging over us."

* Serve as a bridge/transition

Just as narrative can serve as a transition between events, so dialogue may serve as a bridge to move from one idea or event to another. In the following example, the opening narrative offers a summary of information about a route soldiers must follow to get to Yorktown. Dialogue between the general and the young, mosquito-bitten drummer reveals information and advances the story. Your readers learn about a complication as the characters speak. The mosquitoes are troublesome; the drummer's fingers and hands are swelling so badly that he cannot do his job. Narrative continues to move the story with a description of another complication, the arrival of bad weather.

> The general did not seem concerned that the scouting reports indicated a large salt marsh area his soldiers had to ford as they followed the river during the march from Williamsburg to Yorktown. A large military battle was coming, but nobody, not even the general, knew the natural dangers that lay ahead as the soldiers set out. It was mid-October and unusually warm. Swarms of salt marsh mosquitoes began their feast. The huge mosquitoes attacked faces, necks, hands and every area of the soldiers' exposed flesh. The young drummer tried to beat the marching cadence with hands that were black with the swarming insects.
>
> "Increase the cadence," the general commanded. There was silence. Not a drumbeat to be heard. "Increase the cadence. That's an order!" The general bellowed his instructions and in an unusual move from the rear, guided his horse to the lagging drummer.
>
> "Sir" the drummer said, holding his hands for the general to inspect, his fingers fat as sausages. "My hands are swelled, and I am unable to hold the drumsticks."
>
> The general shook his head at the pathetic drummer. "Carry on when you are able. Until that

time, I will see that someone calls cadence."

After he ordered the captain to call marching cadence for the soldiers, the general rode to the rear of the column. As he turned his face towards the gray, afternoon sky he felt warm drops of rain. It was gentle at first and welcome, but as the wind shifted to the northeast, the rain turned cold and blew sideways. As they moved towards their destination, the itchy, shivering soldiers tried to remain erect against the elements.

About Speech Tags

You are comfortable having your people talk with each other, but now another problem looms on the horizon. It is characterizing the dialogue or adding speech tags. Characterizing the dialogue does not mean describing your character. This is the step in dialogue where everything can go wrong if characterization is not handled correctly. Speech tags help to inform your readers as to exactly who is speaking. If the character's personality is clearly defined through speech patterns, gestures, etc., a tag may not be needed at all. There seems to no absolutes, no definitive guidelines as to when to use "said", other identifying tags, or nothing. Beginning writers worry about frequent use of "said" during dialogue, to the point that they substitute words which diminish the energy and the natural flow of dialogue. In this example "said" is used, and it works.

"Jessie, please help carry the groceries from the car to the kitchen," Mother said. "Everything is in the trunk."

"In a minute."

10 - Speak to Me

Mother remained calm and said again, "I am asking you a second time. Please help carry the groceries from the car to the kitchen."

"Come on, Mom. Just let me finish the video game."

"JESSIE!"

Jessie's face looked as if he were in pain. "I'm coming," he said.

In the following example, look at the common substitutions for "said," which *don't work*:

"Hello," said Thomas.

"Hello," Rebecca laughed.

"Busy tonight?" queried Thomas.

"No," answered Rebecca.

"How about going to the theater?" Thomas inquired.

"Thought you'd never ask!" exclaimed Rebecca.

"Don't wear anything that is less than elegant," Thomas expostulated.

"How about my new blue chiffon dress?" Rebecca proposed.

"Yes," Thomas happily responded.

Do you see why the tags like "laughed", "queried", "proposed", etc., don't work? They are verbs. Rebecca doesn't laugh her words. Perhaps you could inject a bit of narrative and say Rebecca laughed as she greeted Thomas. She also does not possess the abil-

119

ity to complain words. Laughing and complaining are actions that should be shown to your readers rather than told. Are you confused? Don't be. Chapter Eleven is devoted entirely to the topic of "showing not telling."

Used sparingly, the following words may be substituted for "said:"
added
asked
replied

"I see you found something to take the itch from the insect bites," the general said to the young drummer.

"Well sir," he replied, "I smeared marsh mud on my hands, and that helps." The young drummer looked at the welts rising on the general's neck and added, "Sir, perhaps the mud will work for you."

Another unsuccessful technique is tacking adverbs on to the verb that isn't working. The "ly" offense enters the picture if Rebecca says "Hello" laughingly. There are very few occasions where adverbs enhance "said," so avoid tacking the "ly" words on to "said"

You have seen some examples that work and some that do not work. Here are general guidelines and a few helpful tips for using "said:"

* When a tag is required, "said" should be used about three quarters of the time.
* If you are indecisive about using "said," leave it out. Chances are, you don't need it.
* In dialogue between two characters, use "said" with one character and nothing with the other.

Be of good cheer! There are ways to identify the speaker

without using "said." Action by the person who is speaking, injected in the same paragraph as the quote, identifies the speaker, adds visual information, and can indicate a pause. Your reader is more likely to become involved when provided with an active image along with the dialogue:

Action followed by dialogue:

> Joey stood up and reached across the table for the car keys, "I'm out of here. I've got places to go, people to see."
>
> "You can't leave yet. We haven't had dessert," Melinda said.

Joey's action gives a hint of his character before he ever says a word. "Said" is unnecessary for Joey but is necessary to identify Melinda.

Action interjected in dialogue:

> "Just think—" Paul leaned back in his chair contemplating the small white paper, "I could be the next lottery winner with this ticket."

A pause, a break in the dialogue

Breaks in the dialogue may be used effectively to identify way that a character feels. This assists your readers without having to say that he paused for a moment before he spoke, etc. Inserting the action creates the pause. With brief pauses you can create a flow, a rhythm in the dialogue.

Keeper of the Stories

There is a downside. If you overuse the pause technique you may create choppy dialogue. Any potential for lively dialogue is lost in the following example:

"Just think—" Paul leaned back in his chair contemplating the small white paper. "I could be the next lottery winner with this ticket."

Jasmine ran water in the sink to do dishes. "What is the jackpot now?" She moved her hands around in the soapy water.

Paul closed his eyes and put his hands behind his head. He thought of being rich. "It might be million or so."

She picked at the egg yolk, bonded to the blue and white plate. "If you win, could we get new dishes?" She put the plate in the water to soak.

Paul took off his shoes and studied the holes in the toes of both socks. "Maybe I'll get a new pair of socks."

* Questions

To write dialogue without any "saids" would be like writing a movie script. Since your story is not visual the way a play is, with actors moving about, how do you know who is speaking? The question and answer technique requires careful planning, but can work.

"Why are you standing on my front porch?" Sylvia asks.

"I've come for the wedding reception."

"Should I recognize you? What's your name?"

"Robert James."

"No way! My sister dumped you years ago."

"That's what she wants everyone to believe."

Reading the work of emerging writers as well as that of established ones is an interesting way to keep current with what is happening in writing community. However, it has been my experience that the best way to write good dialogue is to write and write dialogue. Working on a writing technique is like vowing to become physically fit. The more you exercise, the more fit you become. So flex your dialogue-writing muscles. As a beginning, sit in the mall and listen to conversations. While you are waiting in a checkout line, eavesdrop on the conversation behind your or in the next checkout lane. At the next gathering, listen to the family conversations.

East Tennessee poet and playwright Jo Carson listened to people and found stories in their casual conversations. Her book, *Stories I Ain't Told Nobody Yet* (Theater Communications Group, 1991), is a collection of monologues and dialogues she has written from conversations she has overheard. This interesting book is part of an ongoing work, *People Places*. Not only should you read *Stories I Ain't Told Nobody Yet* for pure pleasure, but also by reading it, you will see good examples of informal conversational dialogue. She has captured flavor of the Appalachian region, the rhythm of life, and speech patterns of East Tennessee.

Notes

CHAPTER ELEVEN:
Show, Don't Tell

How in the world do you show something without telling about it? Do you recall "Show and Tell" Fridays in the primary grades? Perhaps after thoughtful consideration or total mayhem searching for something, anything, there you stood in front of the class with an item. You were expected to explain and when necessary demonstrate the item.

Long ago, when I was in elementary school, it was an era of fly-by-night circuses that sold small exotic pets. Chameleons were popular and indeed one of my classmates brought her circus pet to school for "Show and Tell." She told us he would change color, and he did. We had hoped for pink or violet, but we were satisfied that he did indeed take on the color characteristics wherever he was placed.

The young man who brought a test tube of mercury showed us the substance, shook the tube, and declared that if it ever spilled it would go into a hundred million little sliver balls. We didn't believe his claim because we didn't see it spill and splatter. Later in the school day, quite by "accident" a doubter unleashed the tube of mercury, and we scrambled from our desks, tipping them as we fell to our knees to see the little balls of mercury. Any motion at all made them roll.

Most of all, my classmates did not believe the young man who proclaimed during "Show and Tell" each Friday that his entire basement was filled with train track, little villages, people, trees, blinking crossing signals, and three eight-car trains. Each week he had a new installment to his train story. He told us in detail how he and his father created the trees from sponges, made the surfaces for the track, and did all the electrical wiring.

And so it went, week after week he droned on and on completely absorbed in his train world. I knew he was telling the truth because he lived up the street from me, and I had been to the basement and seen the trains run through tunnels, whistle as they cross trestles, and safety gates go down at crossings as the trains moved through the villages and countryside. The other kids had not been to his basement, and to them, his talk was boring. The teacher suggested that he bring in something related to his trains for the class to see. The next Friday, he wore a black and white striped engineer's hat as he talked. While they ran the trains, he and his dad wore matching engineer hats. The class still couldn't visualize the train city setup, until the field trip to his house when they saw it all.

It is your job as the writer to be the camera, to help your readers see it all. One of my students who uses the *nom de plume* John Sampson, wrote a humorous narrative showing us his garage through a "show don't tell" exercise. I offered the following telling sentence to the class: "The garage was a mess." Sampson describes the general clutter and then becomes specific as he examines the curious assortment of goods collecting their "patina of neglect." As he describes in detail the messy workbench, detail-by-detail, he builds interest, and weaves his story.

The high point of the story is the accidental demise of two special flower arrangements. As you read his story based on the telling sentence describing in detail the interior of the garage, observe how he also reveals a gentle, subtle story of family dynamics. The way husband and wife divide their space and feel about that space is revealed in the piece.

SHAMROCKS AND ROSES
by
John Sampson

My stomach churns as I view the garage from the top stair. The garage is a mess, as Tallulah Bankhead would say, "A Cinci-God-damned-nati mess." This unloved, uncared-for, neglected space is crammed with ripening junk . . . things we are unable to put in the garbage, things that need to collect a few years of dust and rust so we will feel justified when we throw them out. As my eyes wander over the garage, they fall on the cobweb and dust covered Magic Carpet Shampooer bought fifteen years ago, the rusty hand-pushed lawn mower purchased thirty years ago. Then there are the dusty vases, pitchers, urns, baskets, planters, jardinieres, cooking pots, cookie sheets, cake pans and a waffle iron; all gathering their patina of neglect. When did we last use any of them? But these are orderly compared to the jumble of cardboard boxes that nearly engulf the workbench. I started to tear the boxes up for recycling after Christmas when Rhoda's voice flooded back into my consciousness, "John, I need that Nordstrom's box from the garage, the one my black pumps came in."

I again remembered the flush of guilt that swept over me that October morning remembering I had recycled that box six months earlier in March.

"Will another box do?" I asked.

So today, I must thread my way through Rhoda's boxes, recalling each Christmas gift it had brought. Large boxes were for the heavy stone hedgehog, bronze garden lanterns and ceramic rooster. Smaller boxes housed turtle night lights with then glistening green shells, books, and oversized TV remote controllers and small boxes for tooth-sucking Guava jams and jellies from Hawaii, lingonberry jam and syrups from Scandinavia, smoked salmon from Alaska, melt-in-your-mouth frangoes from Seattle, sticky sweet fruitcake from Texas, and from Amish country sterilized manure gargoyle and snail to make the flowers grow. But topping all this were the other boxes that arrived at 59 Belvedere Drive laden with Christmas gifts for our four sons and families who were with us over the Christmas holiday.

Now on this day, March 10, I must clear some floor space in the guest bedroom as our son, Josh, will be visiting this weekend. The table and shamrocks that occupy that floor space will have to go. I

11 - Show, Don't Tell

stash the table on the front porch with the lawn chairs, but it is too cold to put the shamrock outside. "Where can I put it?" I think. "In the garage, on the workbench in front of the window, that's the place for it."

So here I am, stomach churning, standing on the top step to the garage surveying the workbench and realizing this may not be an easy task. Peering over the boxes, I see the oversized fishbowl of Acuba that I put on the window end of the workbench to root. And I also see the enormous bouquets of pink and red roses, two giant masses of color. While they are beautiful, recalling all the freshness or summer, and I can almost smell their fragrance, they are taking up most of the remaining workbench space. Rhoda told me they were there but I had forgotten. She also told me how long she worked to arrange them in just the right shape for their Easter debut at the cemetery.

With shamrocks in hand I descend the stairway and reach the workbench with only one box falling on my leg. There is no place to put the shamrocks so I slowly slide the Acuba down the workbench with my arm. The Acuba hits the first bouquet of roses knocking it over and it in turn topples the second bouquet of roses, but there is now room to put the shamrock on the bench. With both hands free, I get the roses up but they fall over again. With great care I finally get them to remain standing. They are lopsided. The roses have a definite port list. I pat them with both hands to restore their lost roundness, but much as I try, they are still off balance. Then I tread my way through the boxes and back to the safety of Rhoda's orderly house.

******

"Rhoda, I have just finished my garage is a mess story. Will you read it?" I ask as Rhoda passes my study door. "Any comments will be appreciated."

"I suppose it is about my roses."

"Well, yes it is." She takes the story and disappears down the hall.

Rhoda reappears, her face is flushed. "This isn't right! You talk about my things in the garage, and there's nothing about your things, like all those shelves of hazardous products you have out there."

"What hazardous products?"

"All those gallons of old house paint. If you threw them out you could get most of the things up off the floor and on those shelves including the boxes. And what's more, my roses have been in the garage just four days while your mess has been there for forty years."

I blanch. Rhoda is right. Eighty percent of the stuff in the garage is mine. And I hereby resolve to clean it up the day school is out, unless I am too busy in the yard or writing stories like this.

Ann Falcone Shalaski, a writer and member of the LifeLong Learning Society, selected a different telling sentence during the "Show don't Tell" class exercise. "The diner was empty" is the sentence Shalaski chose. The story that came to her is purely fiction; therefore this is not her family's story. However, "The Tennessee Waltz" is the story of family.

Writers are propelled by strong emotion while developing the story; we refer to it as "fire in the belly." It is generally understood among writers that whatever emotions we feel while we compose our stories are translated to become part of the personality or personal energy of our people or characters. Shalaski doesn't *tell* you that The Tennessee Waltz appears to have a message of family disconnect and rivalry. Through detail, she *shows* you. Search beyond the obvious details to the levels of meaning. There is message, which speaks to not taking life or family for granted.

THE TENNESSEE WALTZ

by

Ann Falcone Shalaski

The diner was empty. Easing into a booth, wiping mottled dust from the table, I felt uneasy as the storm continued to hammer the metal roof like kettledrum, and wind slapped waves of rain flooding the grimy windows. Condensation spilled over the sills and down the faded blue walls. Floral plastic curtains, brittle and cracked, did little to improve the bleak surroundings. It was Sunday, a day for families, togetherness and love, not my favorite day.

An ancient jukebox crowded the far corner of the deserted diner. Red and yellow lights glared, like eyes on an overgrown insect. A disheveled wait-

Keeper of the Stories

ress ambled over; Betty was embroidered in black and white thread across her apron.

"We're closed," she said, disdainfully.

I could smell the camphor oil she rubbed all over her chest. Silver crescent moors dangled from her ears, clinking like wind chimes when she moved her head.

"I'm sorry," I said, preparing to leave. "I saw the lights on and the front door was open."

"Wait," her voice softened. "You can stay, it isn't safe to leave right now." She motioned for me to sit. "I'll get the cook. He'll fix some eggs." Patting her overly permed gray hair, and leaning against the booth, she reminded me of a fading kewpie doll with thick blue eye shadow and pale chalky skin.

I hesitated. "Eggs would be fine, thanks, Betty." I was grateful she changed her mind. Coffee and conversation would help until the rain passed. I paled when a grumpy man with a huge neck approached.

"That's my brother, Henry, the cook," Betty explained. "Henry Berman has the personality of a lizard."

Henry lumbered like a field hand. His too-short white pants, short-sleeve white shirt, and half apron were dingy and stained. I could see that Henry had wiped his hands many times on his apron. His big palm prints covered the seat of his white pants.

I glanced at the rows of jelly glasses, brown

jugs, and thick mason jars lining the top shelf of the diner. On a smaller shelf over the grille was a bronze clock with a lion on top. A faded black and white photograph and a vase of dried hydrangeas completed the display.

I studied the gilt-framed photograph, "Berman's Family Diner, Established, 1945" was the caption. A smiling, proud man, tall and handsome, with dark hair that lifted from his forehead, held a young girl's hand. The girl's skin was pale and tendril-like curls framed her face. The girl's arm was extended and rested on the shoulder of a lanky boy. The boy, her brother, I guessed, had dark, deep-set eyes, gangling hands and very large feet.

The refrigerator door swished then moaned shut. "Yaw want fried or scrambled?" Henry asked, holding a wire basket to his chest. Selecting three eggs from the pyramid, he cracked them simultaneously. Henry palmed the shells and pulverized them in his fist. Betty flinched, I heard Henry snicker behind his bear-sized fist.

"What's your name?" Betty asked.

"Marlese," I said, still distracted by Henry's unpleasant behavior.

"Not much traffic on Main Street, especially on Sundays." Betty chattered on. "Makes it easier to get around those damn railroad tracks."

I turned to look at her. She had one hand on her hip and the other pressed to her chest.

My mouth felt dry; I struggled to speak. Betty's expression never changed. "The railroad tracks are gone. They were pulled up years ago."

"Well, I don't drive, not since my Buick broke down." Betty gestured with her thumb to the back window of the diner. "Besides, I gotta keep my eyes on things in here, every minute."

I could see Betty's car from the window, a 1955 Buick Roadmaster. It was over forty years old. I shuddered. The diner smelled of old age and sadness.

"Fix her eggs nice and fluffy, Henry, and use the good oleo." Betty put silverware and napkins on the table. I grew uncomfortable as she slammed drawers; her voice was strained and low. "I'm sick and tired of your penny-pinching thievery. Holding on to every cent so you can have it all for yourself. If Papa only knew the kind of son you've become! Bless his soul," Betty added, as an afterthought.

Henry's face flushed, his brow bristled, his chest burst out of his shirt. "I'm the second Henry Berman," he said, wedging his body between Betty and the counter, eyeing me suspiciously. "This diner is mine, from father to son, the way it should be, tradition." Henry paused, his voice fell, "You never worked a day to earn your keep, but Papa couldn't see that. You kept him wrapped around your finger. It won't be long, Betty, my time is coming."

Betty pushed her forefinger in Henry's chest. "I'll see you dead and buried." Her voice was dry as

11 - Show, Don't Tell

dust. "I'll never leave this diner, or you, for one minute. I've waited too long to get what belongs to me."

Henry shrugged, then shuffled away. I assumed he had heard it all before. Henry returned and wistfully pushed a handful of nickels in my direction. "Play the jukebox," he said, "play anything; number eleven is my favorite."

It took a moment for me to respond. Mirrored in their faces, I saw the destructiveness of an unlived life. I felt drained and empty like Betty and Henry and the disintegrating diner. Berman's Diner had music I didn't recognize. "That's My Desire" by Frankie Lane, "Singing the Blues," by Guy Mitchell, and "Tom Dooley," by The Kingston Trio, I played Henry's request, number eleven, "Tennessee Waltz," by Patti Page. It was evident the passage of time stopped long ago, probably when Henry Berman, the patriarch, died. For Betty and Henry every day was yesterday warmed over.

The scent of coffee curled, drawing me back to the booth. Perking brown liquid rattled the tin coffeepot. Betty poured two steaming mugs. The blue veins in her hands curved and crossed, disappearing into trembling fingers. She sighed dispiritedly, then sat.

Henry came to my table with the eggs and overdone toast. "Well, ain't this cozy, you sitting on your hands while I do all the work." He glared at Betty. "You'll have your hand out on payday, won't you Betty?"

Betty recoiled; as her focus returned to me, she wrapped her hands around the coffee mug and ignored Henry. "So, tell me, what do you do? Where do you live? I've never seen you in here before, I would know. Are you married?" she asked.

"I work in pharmaceutical sales. The mid-Atlantic region is my territory," I replied, "I'm not married, I travel most of the time."

"You mean you go from city to city?" Betty asked, amazed. "You go to these places by yourself? You see new people all the time? Oh, my." Betty's voice grew smaller.

"Actually, my work takes me from state to state. I like being independent. I do get back to my apartment, about four days a month."

Betty blinked, and she set her coffee mug on the table. "Wouldn't you rather stay in one place? Be with your family? Have roots?" She pressed me to continue.

"I don't have a family, or a family home to visit; no roots, for that matter. Just a small apartment, a place to keep my stuff and get my mail." I continued buttering my toast.

Betty leaned closer, touching my hand. "How sad for you," she said. "When I was growing up, everyone I knew had a family, and they spent time together. My father, Henry, and my mother, Rose, opened this diner many, many years ago. We lived in the back. Those were the happy days." Betty's voice trailed off. She appeared to be contemplating the only good thing she had left, her childhood memories.

I reached over and touched Betty's arm, Henry's eyes followed me intently. "You have a family. You and Henry area family of two." Pointing to the photograph, I continued, "I see a loving father. Betty, you have roots, a history to be proud of." I watched as Betty pressed her eyes with her apron. Henry's shoulders slumped.

"I would give anything to have had a family. I don't know who my parents are, I don't know who I belong to. No family traditions, no heritage to be proud of."

Henry squeezed into the booth beside Betty. His face was troubled, his eyes dark and lifeless. "You inherited a legacy, and it's not this diner. Rose and Henry Berman left you their love." My voice wavered with emotion. I plunged ahead, carried by a powerful force. "You hoarded it and denied love from each other until your greatest gift died; smothered by suspicion and greed. Wasting your lives, waiting to collect Henry and Rose Berman's inheritance, how sad," I said, "when you've had it all along."

I left the diner. As I pushed the old screen door, raindrops, fragile as spun glass, trickled down my hands. The glistening trails pooled at my fingertips. I felt cleansed and refreshed. Shifting clouds parted. I turned my face to the breaking sun. The air was sweet, alive with sounds of "Tennessee

Waltz." Sunday felt all right.

So, how do you know if or when you are telling or showing? Telling has its place. It is similar to a narrative summary. However, telling can also be vague. Showing is the detail, the clarity.

In "The Tennessee Waltz" Ms. Shalaski brings you one picture after another. She does not settle for telling her readers that the empty diner was old and in bad shape. She shows them. The table wasn't just dirty. It was mottled with dust. The drapes weren't simply made of old plastic. They were brittle and dry. She describes the family picture in detail rather than saying there was an old photograph. Perking brown liquid rattled the tin coffeepot is more effective than telling the reader that Betty made coffee. In telling us of Betty's vintage Buick Roadmaster and the selections on the jukebox, Ann, without hitting the reader over the head with the information, gives a sense of when life went on hold for Betty and Henry.

She also uses similes such as "her voice was as dry as dust," and "raindrops fragile as spun glass." She uses a metaphor to describe Henry's bear-size fist. Through careful verb choice she also achieves her goal of showing not telling. Two examples are: "brow bristles" and "the refrigerator swishes then moans shut."

Lastly, she uses adverbs sparingly. Adverbs such as wistfully and dispiritedly are effective because they are well placed.

In the Appendix you will find more discussion on how to achieve clarity with detail, the use of similes and metaphors as descriptive techniques, and information on how to avoid adverb abuse.

CHAPTER TWELVE:
Donations to the Word Bank

There is good news and bad news as you finish each writing project. The good news is you have reached your goal. The bad news is that it is now time to read your work with a critical eye and possibly rewrite portions of it. In the beginning, my heart was never in the rewrite phase. I thought each sentence was so well crafted that no rewrite would be necessary. But alas, after setting a manuscript aside for a few days, I look at it with fresh eyes and see that perhaps not every word of every sentence is necessary.

Sometimes, to maintain the integrity of the piece, I force myself to cut entire paragraphs of my carefully selected words. I find comfort when I take the attitude that I am making donations to the word bank. My perfectly perfect words aren't discarded, but donated to the great word bank, saved to be recycled at another time for another project.

If you don't have a small grammar handbook tucked away on a shelf, I recommend investing in one. You may wish to refer to the grammar handbook

Keeper of the Stories

in the rewrite phase so you will understand why an error is an error, so you will not continue to make it. Grammar books offer specific explanations, guidelines, and directions for most "situations." Although many computers are equipped with grammar correction, they offer you the solution without a full explanation.

If you had a bad experience with grammar in school, you need not worry. Booksellers everywhere handle good books that are less complicated than college grammar manuals. The reference division of Houghton Mifflin Company offers a small three-volume desk set based on the *New American Heritage Dictionary*. The set contains a spelling dictionary, a concise thesaurus, as well as volume on the mechanics of writing. Another resource is *The Merriam-Webster Concise Handbook for Writers*.

Plan to edit your work in two ways. Put on your editor's cap and review the content of your story to see if you have accomplished what you set out to do, tell a story. If you have not referred to your prewriting cluster ideas or outline, now is the perfect time. Sometimes, ideas change as you are writing. That is fine. If you have strayed from your original plan, did you move in a specific direction, or did you meander your way to the end?

Reading aloud is a good way to uncover problems relating to clarity. Sometimes the fault is not that the story line breaks down, but that the sentence structure is weak. As you revise, keep in mind the following thoughts about sentences:

* Rambling sentences are too long and should be rewritten, becoming two or more sentences.
* Sentences with unnecessary repetition do not move your story along and should be rewritten.
* For examples of faulty sentences, see the Appendix.

12 - Donations to the Word Bank

Word choice is another area that can wreak havoc upon your work. There are several problems that fall in this category:

* Descriptive clutter - Wordiness detracts from the point.
* Redundancy - Say it once and don't take two or more sentences explain what you have just written.
* Adverb overuse - Adverbs used to decorate weak verbs detract.
* Too many similes and metaphors - Too much imagery does not enhance your point.
* Cliché abuse - A story loaded with tired expressions lacks vitality.

These are areas that create the most problems. Again, I refer you to the Appendix for specific examples, and lists of overused words and phrases.

With your grammar handbook at your side, look at the technical aspect. This includes spelling, capitalization, grammar, and punctuation. Here is an all-purpose, troubleshooting checklist to assist you as you edit:

* Check verb tense: Do you inadvertently move past to present and back to past tense in the same sentence?
* Check your verb choice: Are your verbs imprecise, ineffectual or basically weak?
* Check for active voice versus passive voice.
* Punctuation errors - Check comma use. Do too many commas break the flow of the sentence?
* Check punctuation involved with dialogue.
* Check the use of exclamation marks. Too many will detract rather emphasize the points.

In the Appendix you will find examples related to common problems involving verbs, adverbs, and active versus passive voice. There is also a discussion, with samples, of the most common punctuation errors—comma overload.

Often it is beneficial to have a friend read your work and offer constructive criticism. If you ask folks directly related to your story to read it before you believe it is ready, you might set yourself up for controversy and a flurry of their suggested content corrections. Remember, everybody has a version of the truth.

Completing your collection of family stories is like giving birth. The baby you wanted for so long is here; so now what do you do with it? Will you file it in your archives to be discovered after you have departed this earth, or do you wish to present it to family members as a holiday gift or at a family reunion?

You are faced with another question: how do you want your collection of family stories to look? A sheaf of papers tucked in a folder? Think again. You have spent a lot of time and energy on this project. If you prepare your stories for several families, you will need to make copies. What has been a fun project shouldn't end as a copy machine nightmare. Local printers as well as office supply superstores often have reasonable copy rates. Do you resist using copy machines because of bad experiences such as the paper jam, the paper supply run out, or other trouble messages pop up in the view box? Local printers as well as the office supply superstores with copy centers are happy to help. This takes away the mystery and the anxiety of using a copy machine.

If you need assistance with the layout, just ask. They will listen to your ideas, assess your needs, and offer helpful suggestions. Perhaps you would like to include old photos. Once again the copy machine gurus will help you by showing how to copy a picture so that it looks original, without damaging the original. They can offer suggestions on quality or color of paper.

Do you envision your manuscript in a self-cover of heavier paper? For minimal cost, you can go all-out and give your manuscript a professional touch. Many office supply places, large and small, offer binding services. Usually, the choices are spiral binding or a comb binding. They have equipment to punch the exact-space holes and will also insert the spiral or comb. Of course these are not free services. If you want to be cost efficient, shop around. Request estimates from several places.

There are other cover options. Plan to take some time in the office supply store and consider the selections. The covers range from lightweight, plastic see-through covers and fabric ring binders to substantial thesis binders.

I hope in the course of reading this volume you have come to realize that life is a story. Every day is a new story. Peter Stillman, author of *Families Writing* (Writer's Digest Books, 1989), believes that weaving a family story from an event is much more satisfying than a mere explanation of the event. So heed Stillman's idea: observe, and you will realize there are stories yearning to be told. Whenever, wherever families gather, stories are born.

Notes

APPENDIX

Helpful Tips to Consider While Revising Your Work

These suggestions address the problems that plague my students' written work repeatedly. The following guidelines are general. Consult a writer's resource guide such as *The Practical English Handbook* by Houghton Mifflin Company, or their desk series based on *The New American Heritage Dictionary* or *The Merriam-Webster Concise Handbook for Writers* to answer questions, and to read rules that govern specific problems or situations.

More About Sentences
* The length of your sentence depends upon your purpose. There is no rule that says seven words is a good number but fifteen exceeds the limit. But sentences can get out of control in several ways:

* Rambling sentences lose your readers' interest. An example of a rambling sentence:

> Edna's grandchildren made a mess at her sixtieth birthday party, and they ran around the living room popping balloons, and even worse than

that, they spilled lemonade and ice cream on the carpet.

To correct the rambling sentence, break it into two sentences:

> Edna's grandchildren made a mess at her sixtieth birthday party. As they ran around the living room popping balloons, they spilled lemonade and ice cream on the carpet.

Or, try breaking the rambling sentence into three sentences:

> Edna's grandchildren made a mess at her sixtieth birthday party. They ran around the living room popping balloons. They spilled lemonade and ice cream on the carpet.

* Repetitive sentences are weakened when an idea is re-explained after it has already been expressed. Here is an example of a repetitive sentence:

> My mother has a summer vacation home at the beach that is a wonderful vacation place to meet her visiting relatives.

To streamline the repetitive sentence, eliminate some words:

> My mother's summer home at the beach is a wonderful place to meet vacationing relatives.

More About Word Choice:

* Descriptive clutter - wordiness detracts from your point. One good descriptive phrase will make your point:

> The condition of our late grandfather's old abandoned, derelict, firetrap house concerned us.

Remove the descriptive clutter and the point is clear:

> Our late grandfather's abandoned house was a firetrap, and we were concerned.

or,

> We were concerned that our late grandfather's abandoned house was a firetrap.

* Literary device overload: literary devices sprinkled throughout a work are wonderful when used wisely and in moderation. If you include too many overused literary devices, though, your readers may find the material boring, and they might not make it to the end of your thoughtfully crafted story. No doubt you were introduced to literary devices in fourth or fifth grade. You were told that a simile is a comparison of two things using "like" or "as," a metaphor is a comparison of two things without using "like" or "as," and personification is bringing life to an inanimate object. Did you keep a simile notebook? "He moves like greased lightening" and "she is pretty as a picture" are classic and exhausted similes. Metaphors were tricky, but personification was always interesting. Perhaps

"the wind whistled" or a similar one is the first personification example that locked the concept into your literary brain as it did in mine.

In the following samples, you will see one way to energize a tired simile:

> He was as hungry as a bear.
>
> He was as hungry as a sleepy bear that had hibernated until summer.

Change the bear image to a metaphor:

> It is two in the morning, and Joe can not sleep. He is a starving bear, prowling around the kitchen for food.

To personify hunger and carry the bear you could write the following:

> Joe skipped lunch. By mid-afternoon, he was a starving bear just out of hibernation. Everyone at the meeting heard the loud, hungry growl from his empty stomach.

* Clichés stand on their own tired feet, but they also surface as tag-along cousins to similes. You will "get the picture" when you check the samples:

> Blushing bride
> Green with envy
> To make a long story short
> White as a sheet
> Busy as a bee
> Cold as ice
> Poor as a church mouse

Appendix

* Hyperbole and idioms may be used in moderation to add interest to your writing. Hyperboles exaggerate an idea while idioms are expressions that have evolved over time. The word cluster of the idiom should be understood as the meaning of a single word. Obviously, the hyperbole and the idiom have their places but are not to be taken literally.

Hyperbole
> The plate broke into a hundred million pieces
> The dishes were plied a mile high in the sink.
> He was glued to the spot.
> The lost child cried his eyes out.
> The dog barked its head off.

Idiom
> Quit pulling my leg.
> It's raining cats and dogs.
> He is off his rocker.
> Plans are still up in the air.
> She's up the creek without a paddle.

* Redundant words and phrases have their place in descriptive clutter, and when not kept in check, could build into redundant sentences. Humor and dramatic impact are easily swallowed in mediocrity. Although these are familiar phrases, they are redundant:

the honest truth - Anything honest is the truth.
foreign imports - An import is not an import unless brought into one country from another.
green in color - Green is the name of a color.
totally unanimous - Unless all agree, it is not unanimous.
ten in number - Ten is a number.
past history - To be history, it has to be in the past.

Keeper of the Stories

* Adverb overuse - adverbs ("ly" words, like "sadly") used to decorate weak verbs detract from your meaning. An adverb's function is to enhance a verb by telling when, where, or how something was or is being done.

Read the following sentences, eliminating the adverbs. Look for another way to indicate the intended emotion. You might consider rewriting the entire sentence.

"I broke my toy airplane," my grandson said sadly.

Here is a way to correct the above sentence by "showing" rather than "telling" that the boy was sad:

He sniffed and blinked back the tears as he cradled the pieces of the toy airplane in his hands. "I broke my toy airplane, Grandpa."

In the next sentence "hardly wait" and "eagerly" are redundant. If one can hardly wait, one is eager:

He said eagerly, "I can hardly wait for the seafood buffet."

The following sentence demonstrates his eagerness and hunger:

"I have been waiting for this seafood buffet," he said as he tucked the checkered napkin under his chin.

Here is another adverb abuse sample leading to a lethargic sentence:

> "I don't know if I should open the door," elderly woman said weakly and apprehensively.

Once again, showing her apprehension is better than telling us she is weak and apprehensive:

> Her hand quivered as she withdrew it, then once more grasped the deadbolt lock. "I don't know if I should open the door," the elderly woman said.

* Weak verbs can be a result of adverb abuse. Adverbs are a tempting way to invigorate a weak verb:

> Sherlock Holmes carefully looked at the bloodstained document.

Drop the adverb and replace the weak verb with a stronger verb. The result is a more interesting sentence.

> Sherlock Holmes scrutinized the bloodstained document.

There are many clutter problems in the next sentence:

> General Green spoke in an extremely loud and angry voice that he directed at the troops.

Strip the sentence of extremely loud and angry voice. These words are supposed to give importance to spoke. Here is a concise way to show that General Green is angry, he is loud, and he is addressing the troops.

> The angry general bellowed orders at his troops.

Keeper of the Stories

Do you see how a few well-chosen words can make the difference?

You can achieve detail and clarity, and avoid clutter, rejuvenating a tired sentence by adding carefully chosen words. In the following sentence look at the pronoun-subject, look at the verb, and look at the overall sentence structure:

>She went to the store to buy milk.

Replace the pronoun with a noun.

>The girl went to the store to buy milk.

That doesn't work very well. Describe the child.

>The curly-haired girl in the yellow sun dress went to the store to buy milk.

What about the verb? "Went" lacks excitement. Surely a stronger verb could put pizzazz into the sentence:

>Her curls bounced as the girl in the yellow sun dress skipped to the store to buy milk.

Play with the sentence so it is no longer a telling sentence but a showing sentence:

>With curls bouncing the girl in the yellow sun dress skipped the cracks in the sidewalk on her way to the store to buy a half-gallon of chocolate milk.

* Verbs in the active voice, versus verbs in the pas-

Appendix

sive voice can pose the last but nevertheless major problem for writers, especially beginning writers. Active voice expresses an action performed by its subject.

>Lightning struck the barn

>(active voice}

Lightning is the subject. The barn is the object that receives the action.

>The barn was struck by lightning

>(passive voice)

Note the change in the following sentence as the verb is changed from passive to active. With the verb in active voice, the sentence is strengthened.

>Ten pancakes were eaten by Jack.

>(passive voice)

>Jack ate ten pancakes.

>(active voice)

Here is a monotonous sentence written in passive voice:

>The basketball game was won by the Falcon Senior Stars when a three-point shot was made at the buzzer by Uncle Billy Brown.

Move into active voice and resuscitate the sentence:

Uncle Billy Brown won the basketball game for the Falcon Senior Stars by hitting a three point shot at the buzzer.

More About Punctuation

The following points represent frequent comma errors in prose writing. This is not a complete list of when—and when not—to use commas. Please check a grammar and punctuation handbook for a thorough discussion of commas.

* Use commas to set off Items in a series:

    Al misplaced his hat, gloves, and keys.

* Use a comma to separate compound modifiers:

    He laughed in a loud, obnoxious way.

* Use a comma to set off words in direct address:

    That question, Mr. Jones, is unanswerable.

Another example:

    Mr. Jones, that question is unanswerable.

* Use a comma to set off a mild exclamation:

    Oh my, what a beautiful sunset!

* Use a comma to set off transitional words such as

"however," "finally," and "meanwhile"

Finally, Joe turned to the classified ads to find a job.

Punctuating Dialogue
* Use a comma to separate the speaker from what is said. Use quotation marks to set off what is said:

Jill said, "I lost my dog."

Another example:

"I lost my dog," Jill said.

Another example:

"My dog," Jill said, "is lost."

* Always place the sentence end punctuation within the quotation marks.

Jill said, "I lost my dog." (correct)

Jill said, "I lost my dog". (incorrect)

Keeper of the Stories

Diagram

Sunburst Cluster

Appendix

Diagram

Family Tree

Keeper of the Stories

Life Questions

Here is an exercise in the form of a questionnaire for you or others to complete. The suggestions require some thought, and the results may be surprising. It is a good tool for developing insight within yourself as well as in others while you gather information and stories. Write on a separate piece of paper, for it is difficult to write thoughtful answers in small spaces.

1. My three wishes are

_____

_____

_____

2. I consider myself

_____

3. In the mirror I see

_____

4. What I hope people remember about me is

_____

5. I know how to

_____

6. People always ask me

_____

7. My answer is

8. I don't care if I never attend another

9. I laugh when

10. I am sad when

11. Someday I will learn to

12. There is nothing that scares me more than

13. I enjoy eating

14. I will never forget the time

15. This time next year I

BOOKS FOR ADDITIONAL READING

Adams, Sheila Kay. *Come Go Home With Me.* Chapel Hill, NC: The University of North Carolina Press, 1995.

Brohaugh, William. *Write Tight.* Cincinnati, OH: Writer's Digest Books, 1993.

Carson, Jo. *Stories I Ain't Told Nobody Yet.* New York, NY: Theater Communications Group, 1991.

Conway, Jill Ker. *When Memory Speaks.* New York, NY: Alfred A. Knopf, Inc., 1998.

Giovanni, Nikki. *Grand Fathers: Reminiscences, Poems, Recipes, And Photos Of The Keepers Of Our Traditions.* New York, NY: Henry Holt and Company, 1999.

Giovanni, Nikki. *Grand Mothers: Poems, Reminiscences, and Short Stories About the Keepers of Our Traditions.* New York, NY: Henry Holt and Company, 1994.

Greer, Bob and Fulgord, D.G. *To Our Children's Children, Preserving Family History for Generations to Come.* New York, NY: Doubleday, 1993.

Hague, Richard. *Milltown Natural.* Huron, OH: Bottom Dog Press, 1997.

Ledoux, Denis. *Turning Memories into Memoirs, A Handbook for Writing Lifestories.* Lisbon Falls, ME: Soleil Press, 1993.

McDowell, Deborah E. *Leaving Pipe Shop.* New York, NY: Scribner, 1996.

Rule, Rebecca and Wheeler, Susan. *True Stories.* Portsmouth, NH: Heinemann, 2000.

Stillman, Peter R. *Families Writing.* Cincinnati, OH: Writer's Digest Books, 1992.

Willard, Jim and Terry. *Ancestors, A Beginners Guide to Family History and Genealogy.* New York, NY: Houghton Mifflin Company, 1997.

Zinsser, William, ed. *Inventing the Truth, The Art and Craft of Memoir.* New York, NY: Mariner Books/Houghton Mifflin Company, 1998.

USEFUL REFERENCE BOOKS

Strunk, William Jr., and White. E.B. *The Elements of Style.* 4th ed. Needham, MA: Allyn & Bacon/Longman, 2000.

The Merriam-Webster Concise Handbook for Writers. Springfield, MA: Merriam-Webster, Inc., 1991.

Watkins, Floyd C. and Dillingham, William B. *Practical English Handbook.* 9th edn Boston, MA: Houghton Mifflin Company, 1992.

Index

A

"About Corsages" (story) 49
Adams, Sheila Kay 43, 76
Anderson Automobiles 47
Anecdotal Stories 7-8, 76
Appalachian Elders--A Warm Hearth Sampler 46
Appalachian Mountains 45
Ask Jeeves 15
Audubon, John James 36
Aunt Emily 6, 24-25, 66-69
Aunt Jane 25

B

Bear Wallow Road 40
Bessemer, AL 47
Big Sandy River 5
Birmingham, AL 48
Blacksburg, VA 45
"Blank page blues" 7, 39
Blue Ridge Parkway 37
Brainstorming techniques 63-65
  See also Sunburst mind-map illustration, 64
Broom-making 38
Bunyan, John 8
Byrd, William 22

C

Carson, Jo 123
Charlottesville, VA 47
Christopher Newport University ix, 3, 7, 21, 37, 48
Church of Jesus Christ of the Latter Day Saints 16
Civil War 12-13, 20
Come Go Home With Me 43, 76
Country Diary of an Edwardian Lady, The 36

D

Defoe, Daniel 86
Dennison, Cathee 45
Dialogue 76, 84, 109ff
  action followed by 121
  action interjected into 121
  conversation 112-113
  dialect 111-112
  establishing a characteristic 114-115
  establishing a setting 114
  moving the plot 115-116
  pause in 121
  providing information 113-114
  punctuation 141, 155
  questions 122-123
  speech tags 118
  transition device 116-118
Diaries 24
      See also Writer's tools: diary *vs* journal
Dogpile 15
"Don't Drop Your Ice Cream" (story) 91-93
Duval, Elsie 48-49, 106
Dylan, Bob 1

E

Editing
  active *vs* passive voice 153-154
  adverb abuse 142, 150-152
  clichés 141
  descriptive clutter 143, 145-147, 152
  hyperbole 149
  literary device overuse 141, 147-148
  outside readers 142
  punctuation 141, 1154-155
  reading aloud 140
  redundancy 141, 149,
  sentences 140
  showing *vs* telling 150-151
  word choice 147-154

Eldon, Dan 41
Eldon, Kathy 41
Electronic search engines 15

F

Families Writing 143
Family history
  church records 20
  courthouse 13, 16, 20
  Internet search 15-17
  interviews 25-26, 30, 43
  school records 19
  software 17
  sources 43
School records. *See* Family History: school records
Family life
  as a source of stories 21-22
  interviews 25, 30
  photographs 29-30, 42
  "group write" 91
Family members in research 18
  creating a profile 19, 24, 30
Family tree 11, 14, 15
  illustrations 14, 156
Family pedigree 13
Finch, Atticus 85
Finch, "Scout" 85
Foxfire 44-45
Friendship 7 (spacecraft) 35

G

Genealogical Research 16
Genealogical societies 17-18
Giovanni, Nikki 45-46
Glenn, John 35
Glenns, VA 6
God's Oddling 56
Google 15
Grand Fathers 46
Grand Mothers 46

Gwaltney, Doris 37

H

Haskett, James 21-22
Hertford, NC 22
Hill, Eleanor 3, 62, 65, 76-77, 84, 107
History of the Dividing Line, The 22
Holden, Edith 36
Hurricane Hugo 36

I

Interviewing 18-19, 25-26, 28-29
   use of tape recorder 27, 30, 43

J

Jenifer Emily 6, 36, 65
Jones, Bob 5
Journal of the Plague Year 86
Journals, family 24
Journals, writers'. *See* Writer's Journals
Journey is the Destination, The 41
Julius Caesar 101

K

Kelly, Robert 4, 48, 51-52, 97-98
Korean War 96

L

Leaving Pipe Shop 47-48
Lee, Harper 85
Letters 7, 12-13, 17-19
Life Questions 158-159
Lifelong Learning Society ix, 3, 7, 8, 9, 21, 37, 48-49, 57, 76, 130

M

Macbeth 101
Macdonald, Martha 37-38, 46-47
Madison County, NC 43

Maness family
  Andy 24, 75
  George 23-24, 26, 103
  Marty 24
  Terry 24
Marietta College 98
Marietta OH 35
McDowell, Deborah 47-48
McKell, KY, High School, 19
Merriam-Webster Concise Handbook for Writers 140, 145
Millennium 101
Missionaries 22
Mormon Family History Library 16
Mourning bonnet 102-103, 105

N

National Genealogical Society 17
National Park Service 21
New American Heritage Dictionary, The 140, 145
Newport News, VA 49
Newspaper Archives 16, 18, 27
Nixon, Richard M. 35
Norton, Dellie Chandler 43
Nostradamus 101

O

Organization of stories
  binders 61-63
  brainstorming 63
    "sunburst" mind-map illustration 64, 157
  chronological approach 59, 86
  form 58
  historical chronology 59
  outlines 57, 65-66
    sentence 68-69
    topic 66-67
  structure 58-59
  thematic approach 62
  timelines 59-61, 62

P

"Pap's Rain Barrel" (story) 77-84, 107
People Places 123
Pilgrim's Progress, The 8
Practical English Handbook, The 145
Primary sources 27

Q

Questions 28-29

R

Rabun Gap, GA 44
Rappahannock Community College 6
"Red Shoes, The" 4, 8
Reminisce magazine 49
Retired Senior Volunteer Program 46
Reuters News Agency 41
Rock Hill, SC 37, 38, 46-47
Roosevelt, Franklin D. 110-111

S

Sampson, John 107, 126-127
School records 19-20
"Seattle Grunge" look 104
Shakespeare, William 101
Shalaski, Ann Falcone 101, 130-131, 138
Shakespeare's Sister 37
"Shamrocks and Roses" (story) 107-108, 127-130
Showing *vs* telling 125ff, 151-152
Sodom, NC 43
Stillman, Peter 143
Stories, beginning of 95ff
  motive/need 99-101
  person portrait 104-105
  prediction 101-102
  setting 97-98
  strong sensory image 98-99
  symbolic object 102-104
Stories, ending of 105
  circular 105-106

epilogue 107-108
open-ended 108
sensory image 106-107
summary 108
surprise 108
trick 108
Stories I Ain't Told Nobody Yet 123
Story telling
  foreshadowing 87
  flashback/remembrance 86
  interior monologue 87
  narration 86-87
  narrative 85-90, 109
  narrator 87-90
    first person 88-90
    omniscient 90
    unreliable 88-89
Stuart, Jesse 5, 19

T

Tacoma, WA 51-52, 97-98
Tea Cakes and Trolley Rides 37, 46-47
"Tea Time - Aunt Emily's Way" (story) 65, 69-74
"Tennessee Waltz, The" (story) 101, 131-138
Think List 30–32
"Thunder in the Basement" (story) 52-56, 97
Titanic, HMMS 58
To Kill a Mockingbird 85

U

University of Virginia 47

V

Virginia Polytechnic Institute 45

W

War museums 20
War historians 20
Warm Hearth Retirement Community 45
Wheelbarrow memory 23

Wheeling, WV 44
Wigginton, Eliot 44-45
William and Mary, College of 46
Williamsburg, VA 46
Wilmington, NC 36
Woiwode, Larry 22
World War II 5, 22
Writer's block 39
   See also "Blank page blues"
Writer's journal 33, 35, 39
Writer's tools 8, 9, 35, 38, 108
   journals
      binders 2, 40
      diary *vs* journal 33-35
      dream journal 37
      thematic journal 35-36
      weather journal 36-37

Y

YCSSOYF 26
Yorktown, VA 21, 44

Printed in the United States
5005